D0801633

To Come Alive!

A PROJECT TEST PATTERN BOOK
IN PARISH DEVELOPMENT

HARPER & ROW, PUBLISHERS

New York, Evanston, San Francisco, London

JAMES D. ANDERSON

TO COME ALIVE!

*New Proposal for Revitalizing
the Local Church*

TO COME ALIVE! Copyright © 1973 by James D. Anderson All rights reserved. Printed in the United States of America. No part of this book may be used or reproduced in any manner whatsoever without written permission except in the case of brief quotations embodied in critical articles and reviews. For information address Harper & Row, Publishers, Inc., 10 East 25rd Street, New York, N.Y. 10022. Published simultaneously in Canada by Fitzhenry & Whiteside Limited, Toronto.

Designed by Patricia G. Dunbar

Library of Congress Cataloging in Publication Data

Anderson, James D.
  To come alive!
  Includes bibliographical references.
    1. Church renewal. 2. Sociology, Christian.
I. Title.
BV600.2.A5   1973   254   72-11351
ISBN 0-06-060234-1

Contents

Acknowledgments

This book is the result of ten years in the ordained ministry—five in the parish and five as a diocesan staff person. It is the product of reflection upon the totality of that experience in my work, in my family, and with my friends. I believe in a learning process characterized by guided reflection upon experience. A vast array of colleagues and friends have helped to provide the experience and the guidance. That process has continued during the writing of this book. I have drawn heavily upon the wisdom and experience of many people in this attempt to comprehend more fully the complexities of institutional life today. To go through the total list would bore—perhaps confuse—rather than enlighten the reader. What is important is my gratitude to those many persons and my belief that without these multiple relationships life and learning would not be possible for me in any institution.

Project Test Pattern is a national research effort of the Episcopal Church to study the renewal of the local congregation. Its director, is the Rev. Loren Mead. The research files of Project Test Pattern, the support of those involved in the project, and alliances which the project has made possible were indispensable to me.

Trinity Church, New York provided a generous financial grant which I also found indispensable.

My boss and friend, the Rt. Rev. William F. Creighton, Bishop of the Diocese of Washington, gave me time to write this book as well as being one of these many people who have helped make the experience and learning possible. I like the fact that a book about institutional renewal has been written by a member of the institution, on time generously provided by the institution, using monies granted by the institution, and supported by a research project funded by the institution. My experience is of hope realized, and I rejoice in the excitement this experience has brought me.

"Wait, let me tell you what I think. I think that if the beast who sleeps in man could be held down by threats—any kind of threat, whether of jail or of retribution after death—then the highest emblem of humanity would be the lion tamer in the circus with his whip, not the prophet who sacrified himself. But don't you see, this is just the point—what has for centuries raised man above the beast is not the cudgel but an inward music: the irresistible power of unarmed truth, the powerful attraction of its example. It has always been assumed that the most important things in the Gospel are the ethical maxims and commandments. But for me the most important thing is that Christ speaks in parables taken from life, that He explains the truth in terms of everyday reality. The idea that underlies this is that communion between mortals is immortal, and that the whole of life is symbolic because it is meaningful."

—Boris Pasternak, *Dr. Zhivago.*

1

A Ministry to Institutions

A PARADIGM

The institution is the frontier. As the great ancient institutions of our society struggle to maintain themselves it has become apparent that the men and women who labor for the renewal and health of the church, for education, the military, and the corporation, are the individuals moving furthest into the uncharted waters of change in our society.

It was the second of two lengthy meetings in the well-charted vastness of the Pentagon. Three clergy and six military officers drawn together by a deep bond. Our theme centered on the fact that we were key representatives of two of the most ancient organized institutions in society. The soft pastels of the water colors on the walls of the room

where we sat were of combat in the fields and rice paddies of South
Vietnam. We talked of our common problems—the alienation of youth
from our institutions; the ineffectual rigidity of our bureaucracies; the
way in which our systems of promotion, placement, and training failed
to support many of our most competent and innovative men and
women. The clergy had had a good bit of experience in the application
of behavioral science principles and practice to problems such as these.
Many questions were asked about our learning. "What can be done to
help men examine their values and reexamine the nature of their commitment to the institution?" "Is it even possible to make changes from
within, or do we have to create new, parallel, and competing structures
outside the institution?" "Does change have to start at the top with the
general, admiral, or bishop?" "Where does one find the support to
challenge the accepted but no longer effective ways of doing things?"

The clergy mentioned the importance they gave to collegiality—
maintaining working friendships with trusted allies in the fight. One of
the military officers remarked that he felt more personal danger in
working for change and renewal in the Pentagon than he did on the
battlefields of Vietnam! No one laughed. We spoke then of the role
pressures and expectations which an organization can exert on its members—the personal stress and group conflict that occurs in an institution
in tension.

Our talk turned to the basic purpose of our institutions. What does
it mean really to proclaim the gospel of Jesus Christ, or to be an
instrument for the support and execution of the foreign policy of the
United States Government? The authority of our institutions no longer
directs an implicit consensus about our reasons for being. In his leadership role, by what authority does a clergyman or military officer decide
to act for or against the institutional norms?

"I call heaven and earth to witness against you this day, that I have
set before you life and death, blessing and curse; therefore choose life,
that you and your descendents may live. . . . " (Deut 30:19) When
institutions which by their authority have been the transmitters of
standards for discrimination between life and death are themselves

being questioned—when their authority is obviously flawed and under attack—then by what norms does each man choose?

I shared a vision with the group: of the chairman of the Joint Chiefs of Staff debating with the President the purposes our nation would hope to achieve by conventional applications of military force in Vietnam— a conversation which examined the basic ways in which our present conception of the role of the military had contributed to the continuing tragedy of that East Asian country. Is it within the competence and organizational role of a military officer to become involved in matters of policy—and foreign policy? Is it within the competence and organizational role of a clergyman to become involved in political and social issues? We realized that the church has the same difficulty in confronting the fundamental ways in which our conception of religion has supported both just and unjust elements in American life.

Finally we returned to the question of how each man chooses. We agreed that we live in a time of mythic confusion, when the great structures of meaning have seemingly collapsed before our eyes. Then one of the men offered a metaphor of his own. He said that we are immigrants in time, sojourners in the wilderness, wanderers in the desert. He said that such wilderness experiences without secure walls and structures, full of dissent, turmoil, and a search for new gods, was a part of our heritage. I felt a great relief within me as he talked, and sensed the surge of emotion within the room.

As we took our leave and walked down the vast halls of the Pentagon, one of the men turned to me and said, "I feel as if our little band had pitched its tent on a lonely sand dune in the middle of the desert. Suddenly we saw the lights of another group of tents in the gloom—we approached in fear and expectation. I didn't know whether you would be friend or foe—though I hoped you would somehow deliver us from the dangers I faced. But I have found friends and fellow wanderers in the search for truth."

The incident is a paradigm of the themes of this book and the dynamics of institutional life. For this is a story with large dimensions and many rooms. The conversations were born of a desire to:

1. Understand the institution—its nature as an organization—the forces, structures, and processes that shape the life of the institution. To provide this understanding we relied upon our own analyzed experience and knowledge gleaned from the behavioral sciences. Through psychology, psychiatry, sociology, political science, and public and business administration, a body of information has emerged to help us see more clearly the nature of man, his organizations, and the society.

2. Utilize or apply our understanding to the better solution of the overwhelming array of problems facing our institutions.

It was important for us to discuss the values a man holds and the way those values shape his role in the institution. It was also important for us to explore methods for deployment and training of leaders. Institutions today are forced to cope with issues that range from personnel administration to men's systems of belief to the responsibility of the institution in society as a whole. The bridges in man's organizational life between understanding and utilization, between belief and practice, are the themes of this volume.

It is a book for men and women on the frontier of institutional change, and is primarily about the institution "church." I am writing to lay men and women, clergy and practitioners in the behavioral sciences. The intent is to provide a clearer understanding of the church as an organization and to illustrate ways in which that understanding has been used to better resolve our institutional dilemmas. The church *is* an organization, and my hope is to point to these signs that tie daily organizational practices to man's eternal and irresistible search for truth.

Let me be clear that I am not just inquiring into the correlation between the behavioral sciences and the religious enterprise. I am convinced that the core problems in American life are religious, and that those problems are shared—indeed embodied—by our mighty organizations and institutions. The deepest religious questions are not confined to church and synagogue. What do I ground my life in? How can I be free to choose? Where is it all going? Men and women living and working in our great institutions are daily faced with the dilemma of these questions. These dedicated people know that their existence is inextricably bound up with the structures of the institution. They are daily in the fight to take charge of the seemingly rudderless, maniacal drift of the mammoth organizations that shape so much of our destiny. They do not have to be told that these institutions are the organizational embodiment of the attitudes, behavior, and values of a society; they know, because they live it.

I believe that exorcism of the demonic in American life must occur at the level of a ministry to institutions. I am daily engaged in a ministry to the institution—in ways of helping people in organizations find the means of discovering the truth in the everyday reality of their lives. I am not concerned with change or renewal in the usual sense, but with how the church responds to continuing, inevitable change so as to preserve old truths and discard ancient shibboleths. I am concerned with whether or not the church or any other organization can use applied scientific knowledge in ways that recover and prize the recognition of mystery, wonder, and awe in human life. I am caught in the excitement and ferment of raising impertinent questions, conserving essential truths, and releasing people to the freedom of precesses by which they can guide and direct their organizational life.

The first section of the book concerns the particular character of the church as an organization. The middle section addresses itself to specific organizational problems and their resolution. Finally, the third section speaks to the issue of institutional change processes.

APPLIED BEHAVIORAL SCIENCE IN THE CHURCH

The behavioral sciences encompass the fields of psychiatry, psychology, psychoanalysis, social psychology, the management sciences, anthropology, sociology, and the political sciences. It is from this broad range of the social sciences that learnings have been gleaned and applied to the solution of human problems. The movement from theory to application is crucial. That giant step my colleague Bill Yon has called the "so what" step. This is a lovely term: *so what* difference does it make in how I might behave? The practitioner of the applied behavioral sciences is continually translating theory into action. The *so what* question directed to the translation of behavioral science theory into action in the institutional church is at the heart of this book. At the same time I am asking many readers to learn some new words and concepts. These are elements of theory which have proved important to me in understanding the complexities of organizational life.

The application of behavioral science in the American church is not new. Since 1930, with the establishment of the Council for Clinical Training of Theological Students, clergy have increasingly been trained in professional counseling techniques. In 1924 Anton T. Boisen at Worchester State Hospital in Massachusetts began a training program for three seminary students.[1] Today there are over 250 such training centers accredited by the Association for Clinical Pastoral Education. Through direct experience in mental hospitals and other institutions, by guided reflection on that experience, and through study and application of learnings from psychiatry, psychoanalysis, and psychology, the clinical pastoral training movement has exerted great influence on the training of ministerial students. The influence of pastoral training has not been narrowly confined to counseling skills. The self-image of clergy, the processes by which theological education is carried on and the theological understanding of guilt have all been altered by the presence of the clinical training structure in theological education, and this list is far from exhaustive. Yet this enduring marriage between clinical pastoral training and theological education does contain a persistent, unresolved, and often uncreative debate. The debate and its consequences in turn reflect a serious problem within our culture and institutions.

The difficulty is that our culture does not contain a unifying cosmological view. Each of us and each of our institutions is set in the midst of fragmented, dissociated, competing, incongruent, narrowly specialized fields of knowledge. The moment in history when prince and pauper, priest and knight could gaze at the stone arches and mosaics of a cathedral unified in their assumptions about the world is long past. The great structures of meaning have collapsed. Every institution must struggle with a juxtaposition of value differences unparalleled in human history. These differences breed conflict and tension. George Cabot Lodge wrote in 1970 in the *Harvard Business Review*, "The ideological framework that related the timeless values of our western civilization to the real world and guided the activities of our institutions has become palsied and obscure."[2]

Certainly Christianity and behavioral science share a great lack of definition. Martin Luther King and Billy Graham vie in our minds as incarnate symbols of Christian ministry. By the record of their lives and words these men represent competing and conflicting concepts of the Christian faith. A common concept of it does not exist in our culture. I expect local congregations to contain followers of both Billy Graham and Martin Luther King. I expect also to find a third group who are confused by the confusion and do not like either definition. Their confusion is reality-based. It is one of the symptoms of our immigrant —wilderness—status that the institution's authority no longer provides a firm symbolic structure of meaning.

The definition of behavioral science is equally fuzzy. I told a friend this was a book about applied behavioral science. Her disgusted comment was, "Oh—about 'T' groups and *that* kind of thing.' " There is a widespresd assumption that applied behavioral science means sensitivity training, "T" groups, and encounter groups. The church has utilized a wide variety of small-group methods in the past two decades. The mass media have contributed by the attention given to the personal growth centers and the encounter group movement. The result is that group dynamics is a loaded phrase, synonymous with behavioral science and evocative of sensational image. Again the confusion is reality-based. The area of social science is awash with competing theories. Whom are we to believe: Freud or Skinner, Spock or Ann Landers? Group psychotherapy and individual psychoanalysis seem to be more rivals or enemies than collaborating friends.

The scientific contributions to the nature of man are as disparate as are those of the theologians. The academician and the theologian, university and seminary, live under corresponding tension. The *so what* of this particular fact is easy to come by in the practicalities of an organization. When I described this book to a seminary faculty member his first question was, "Will you say anything about the vertical (God) dimension of life or is it all going to be on the horizontal (man) plane?" There are many levels on which the question might be answered—all in some measure reflecting the fact that no one institution and or body of knowledge holds dominion over our hearts and minds.

The question could mean: Am I going to perpetuate the very real separation present in most seminary faculties between the images of the practical, anecdotal, skill-oriented department of Pastoral Theology and the disciplined, academic, heritage-centered, systemic departments of Bible and Theology? The perception of many is that Pastoral Theology —the care of souls—rapidly becomes Pastoral Psychology and is then bastardized into a second-rate psychology. For many church people psychological chauvinism has seemed to eliminate the Divine Presence for a blindly narrow focus on man. For many others the church seems dogmatically transfixed upon the proclamation of a Divine Presence which goes unseen, unheard, unfelt, unknown, unexperienced, and un-realized by growing numbers of people. The organizational rivalry between departments, the personal animosities, the split between reason and revelation, the disjunction between religious and human experience, all continue. The same rivalries and tensions can be paralleled in all our institutions.

On another level the question could be asked: Will I be using religious or psychological jargon? We all dislike jargon. The very word reflects our distaste for narrow, dissociating areas of knowledge. It implies disjunction. It is also a part of our response to the detached, remote technologist from any field. No one wants a cold, scientific technician tinkering with them and their institution. The Dr. Strangelove figure living in servility to the coldly factual side of life is repugnant to us. At the same time, people who live in bureaucracies, whether the church, the military, government, or business, tend to respect credentials. The authority of role is often substituted for that of competence. In the application of behavioral science the church seems to move haphazardly between unthinking rejection of the scientific to uncritical, inappropriate acceptance. My friend and colleague, Dr. Warner Burke, Director of the Center of Organizational Studies at National Training Laboratories, has repeatedly commented to me about this problem. His experience is that churchmen often seem to want to use behavioral science techniques on an emotional feeling plane without the struggle of trying to understand the rationale for choosing an action.

The problem of our response to scientific technology is one of human emotions. I recall the fear and anxiety I felt the first time I submitted to psychological testing. I recall also the tremendous authority I felt in the psychologist's carefully chosen few words of feedback to me.

The behavioral sciences attempt to help us rationally understand our irrationality. As academic disciplines they are a wedding of intellect and emotion. The person attempting to utilize these disciplines in the church needs to recognize that the first reactions of acceptance or rejection are quite likely to be born primarily of feelings internal to the individual's response. It is a level of emotion we all share. Taking into account this form of resistance to the utilization of behavioral science theory in the church, I should like to suggest responding rather with an emphatic listening ear. There is often more feeling to explore than ideology to debate. This is particularly apparent in the way religious experience and terminology have become integrally associated with the history of sensitivity training. As early as 1955 the Episcopal Church committed $350,000 to a large-scale effort to send its clergy through a T group lab experience. The National Council of Churches has officially sponsored Group Life Laboratories since 1954. There are now numerous books available applying group process methodologies to the church. Applications have been widespread and rapid in growth. The encounter group movement has grown almost as rapidly within the church as in the culture as a whole. A large part of the reason for this growth is expressed by Dr. James Clark, Associate Professor of Business Administration at UCLA, in his article entitled "Toward a Theory and Practice of Religious Experiencing."[3] The piece is based on Dr. Clark's extensive experiences as a T group trainer and describes the large numbers of clergy who have expressed their belief that they experienced God in the face-to-face human encounters of a training group. I have been associated for a number of years wtih the Mid-Atlantic Training Committee, an ecumenical organization which has provided sensitivity training as well as training in group leadership and design skills to thousands of clergy and laity. We have come to expect that people will interpret their experiences as being deeply religious and spiritually renewing.

Kurt Back in a recently published interpretive history of sensitivity training states his opinion that the movement occupies a middle ground between religion and science.[4] He interprets the rapid growth of sensitivity training as due to the fact that it fills a primarily religious void in middle-class America. This is a void of personal meaning, deep values, intimate sharing, in short, a hunger for spiritual-personal regeneration: the precise void for which the theology and practice of the church are intended to be witnesses of the Truth.

And so finally the question might mean: Will I use the revered, hallowed words and concepts of the Christian tradition? The answer is Yes. I have learned in psychoanalysis the importance of my own history with its unique words and symbols. The history of a person or an institution embodied in their own language and ideas is of profound importance. On the most elementary level, if a person is not interested in the stuff of my history I feel he may not be interested in me. This is also the way people in the church feel if the intervener is not concerned with the stuff of church history. Does this also mean: will I deal with the sacred, the religious dimension of life? If the reader understands the answer to this question in the narrow, bifurcated terms of most college curriculums then my answer is No. Religious studies as commonly understood mean study of the lore and heritage of the designated organized expressions of religion. Concern with religion and the use of religious language are not synonymous. I am not willing to say that the two meetings at the Pentagon became religious only at the point where the biblical theme of the wilderness was introduced; I believe the meetings were inherently religious—concerned wtih the deeper questions of man's existence: the internal system be which each man chooses what is true or relevant for him, and the way our institutions objectify their own cosmology.

I find that some clergy and laity believe that the peculiar nature of the church places it beyond correlation with other organizations in society. They argue that the supernatural, dynamic, and divine origin of the church leave it essentially without comparison among human institutions. More often I find businessmen and a few behavioral scientists who blithely claim that the problem with the church is that is has not adopted enough of the modern organizational practices of other institutions. The first position claims that only the categories conceived by the church make sense as tools for analysis. The second allows for no significant difference between the phenomena of a business organization and a Presbyterian Synod. In my opinion both views are wrong.

My own position is that the church is a human institution to be studied in the same terms as other social systems. At the same time I believe that it creates situations which are often unique by their prominence and at times unique in their essential setting. I believe this position to be profoundly sacramental. The sharing of bread and wine around a table is an action which occurs in a variety of human settings. It can and must be understood by the same theories and categories as one would comprehend other such examples of feeding, sharing, and ritual. At the same time the sharing of bread and wine in the act of Holy Communion constitutes a set of relationships which are unique to this essential action of the church.

In psychoanalysis one learns that his dreams are imaginative symbols of some piece of truth about himself. Holy Communion is an incarnated symbol of a comprehensive aspect of human existence. By partaking of the reality of one's dreams one is transformed. By partaking of the reality of the Communion one is transformed. There is no transforming without a continued search for understanding. There is no understanding in a passive, cold set of jargon, be it theological or psychological.

The peculiar marks of the church as a corporate body are the sacraments of baptism and Holy Communion. These are objective, living, concrete realities which ground the church in the specificity of human time and event. The revelation of God through the church—the community of the Holy Spirit—is in and through specific recordable phenomena. I believe that the sacramental nature of the church is in fact a faith which makes it imperative for us to comprehend as clearly as possible the behavioral realities of our corporate body.

A MINISTRY TO INSTITUTIONS

The meeting I have described at the Pentagon was focused on the life of two large institutions—the church and the military. For centuries the church has exercised a ministry to individuals in moments of crisis. In recent years emphasis has been placed on a ministry through small groups. The theology and practice of a pastoral ministry to individuals and groups is widely developed and accepted. But there is an equally important ministry to institutions in crisis. The meeting at the Pentagon is one small example of that ministry in action. This book is a step toward the development of a theory and practice of pastoral ministry to institutions.

Jesus reminded his followers that they needed to clear their own vision before attemptiong to remove specks from the eyes of others. The training, competence, and credibility of the pastoral counselor has quite rightly relied heavily upon this advice. In the same vein the institutional church has an obligation to face its own impediments to clear vision.

I have lived for the past several years in proximity to a seminary. One seemingly unchanging characteristic of seminary life is student disappointment over the quality of life found in the seminary community. A recent copy of the student newspaper ran a story in which two students leaving the chapel encounter a dark stranger on the grounds of the seminary. He questions them about their experience of living in a Christian community. The students find themselves answering defensively.

"Strange," reflects the stranger, "as I read in the Bible, Jesus promises strength to overcome sin, something about the Holy Spirit indwelling the lives of Christians and making them new people."

"Right! I can accept that intellectually, but try and live it gut level. It just can't be done, especially here where nobody trusts anybody."

"Well," replies the stranger, "then you are saying that Scripture is wrong or overly idealistic, or are you saying that this is not a Christian community as spoken of in Scripture?"[5]

The dark stranger in the story is, of course, Jesus. The story itself is one of those organizational artifacts which are clues to the quality and nature of the organization's life. The church does, in fact, lay claim to being a forgiving, reconciling, loving community. No matter how often each new generation of seminary students is reminded that the church is made up of fallible, sinful human beings, the expectation continues that the institution will deliver on the promises. Our workaday theology seems to be that the grace of God is powerful enough to renew individuals, but that institutions are hopelessly demonic and sinful. Michael Novak has said that he believes the fundamental problem facing the Christian church today is to discover and decide "which choices of human polity for the structure of a community and for individual life contribute most, over the long run, to fidelity to the revelation of Jesus Chrust."[6]

A ministry to the institution is a ministry addressed to the existing connections between our faith commitments to freedon, love, and justice and the types of social structure, organizational arrangement, and institutional dynamics in which these commitments can be nourished.

The quotation facing page 1 is from the Pantheon edition of Boris Pasternak's *Dr. Zhivago* (New York, 1958), p. 42.

1. Seward Hiltner, ed., *Clinical Pastoral Training* (Commission on Religion and Health of the Federal Council of Churches of Christ in America, 1945), p. 9.

2. George Cabot Lodge, "Top Priority: Renovating Our Ideology," *Harvard Business Review* (September-October 1970), p. 44.

3. Dr. James Clark, "Toward a Theory and Practice of Religious Experiencing," in *Challenges of Humanistic Psychology* James F. T. Bugental, ed. (New York: McGraw-Hill Book Co., 1967), pp. 253–58.

4. Kurt Back, *Beyond Words* (New York: Russell Sage Foundation, 1972), p. 205–6.

5. David Bena, "The Dark Stranger," *AMBO*, "newspaper published by the students of the Protestant Episcopal Theological Seminary in Va." (April 1972), pp. 2–3.

6. Michael Novak, "The Meaning of Church in Anabaptiam and Roman Catholicism Past and Present," in *Voluntary Association*, ed. D. B. Robertson (Richmond, Va.: John Knox Press, 1966), p. 91.

2

The Church as a Social System

To work with an institution you must first understand it. This human understanding of other human beings is tricky business. Ancient Israel had a whole class of honored wise men whose proven gifts were the observation and analysis of human character and conduct. From the dream interpretations of Joseph to Solomon's wise judgment between two women claiming a single living child, the Old Testament bears witness to the need and rarity of a wise understanding of human affairs. "And men came from all peoples to hear the wisdom of Solomon, and from all the kings of the earth, who had heard of his wisdom" (1 Kings 4:34).

Men and women with the authority of wisdom have always been in short supply. Certainly institutions today do not have a class or group

of wise men who are seen as authoritative sources of knowledge about
human conduct. The very state of our understanding of how much we
really know of human affairs is itself chaotic and confusing. I once saw
the chief legislative body of an Episcopal diocese debate for forty-five
minutes—without prior study—the creation of a program to eliminate
racism in the diocese. If the group had been asked to take on the
forty-five minute task of designing (from the transistor up) a new light-
weight portable color-television receiver they would have rejected the
assignment with shouts of laughter. In point of fact, the events of the
last decade have dramatically proven that our technological capacity to
place a man on the moon or to mass-produce television receivers does
not even remotely indicate sufficient wisdom to provide for the social
and communal ills of American life. Because each of us is human, we
do know something of human affairs. I believe with the Bible, however,
that few men are genuinely wise in unraveling the intricacies of human
life.

Men were more certain in ancient times about where to turn for
wisdom. Today the affairs of mankind have been classified and compart-
mentalized, so that the complexity of human conduct is fogged by the
confusion of competing theory and practice. Priest and politician—
Freudian analyst and Skinnerian psychologist—sociologist and philoso-
pher—all have something to say, and each man must decide where he
will find his Solomon. The peculiar end result is that, although very little
is actually known about how human beings live, work, and relate together by comparison, say, with what we know of television, such knowledge as we do have is seldom put to use by our major institutions. The
proliferation of segmented knowledge leads responsible men and women
—allocating precious financial resources—to be each his own Solomon
in matters as to which there is a great deal of information and wisdom
available.

There are some important beginnings in our understanding of organizations. In recent years behavioral science has been grasped by a systems
view of reality. Webster defines a system as an "assemblage of objects
united by some form of regular interaction, combined so as to form an

integral whole." It is the same word and meaning we use in speaking of the digestive system in your body or the mass transit system in your city. To think of systems is to think of the whole, the gestalt, and the dynamic interrelationships among the parts.

To get your mind inside systems thinking, dwell for a moment on our national transportation arrangements. Under President Eisenhower a decision was made to improve vastly one section of our transportation system—the interstate highway network. Only today are the systemic implications of that decision becoming clear. Automobile exhaust pollution, the inadequacy of urban mass transportaion, the meteoric rise of the motel industry, and the diminution of the municipal tax base are only some of the consequences that have flowed from that decision. Transportation turned out to be a systemic problem—an integral whole in which the interaction of the parts brought results no one anticipated. The system turned out to be open to the environment, influenced by and influencing other systems.

An organization on the human scene is a social system. It is a whole —a totality which is more than the sum of its parts, for its wholeness is basic to its interaction with the environment and among its subsystems. A human being is a system. There is no way to understand a single human being by breaking down his body into constituent elements and subsystems. Adding up the chemical elements in his body, together with a long list of subsystems such as the digestive system, nervous system, and skeletal system, just doesn't equal a human being. The reality of that person is found only as we see the whole living person interacting with his environment. The reality of a social system is in its life, its functioning. Contrast this with the purely structural view many of us have of organizations, which leads to the organizational blueprints we call tables of organization—the most common way of describing this type of whole.

The point is crucial. The persistence of our tendency to blueprint organizations as if one could capture the reality by an instant flash picture is pervasive and misleading. Imagine taking a satellite picture from space which would in a single instant capture each and every person and piece of equipment of one of our national airlines. In this marvelous hypothetical photograph one would be able to see the position of every pilot, passenger, executive, stewardess, plane, car, truck, tool, and mechanic. Every person on coffee break and each memo or letter would be captured by the instant all-seeing eye of the satellite. Yet the reality of the airline could not be found in the picture. The reality is in the processes, the dynamics by which that same picture would be unalterably changed an instant later. To see this clearly is to recognize that the focus in understanding organizations must be on the forces that cause the picture to change.

We speak easily of the anatomy of a parish or congregation. In reality it has no anatomy—only a physiology. The structure of a congregation is in the patterns of events and relationships among its members. In this respect a social system differs from a biological system. When a congregation dies there is no body left to dissect. All that remains are artifacts, products of a social system that has disappeared. Archaeologists must base their findings on the products and records of vanished civilizations. The civilization ceases to exist when it stops functioning.

Here is an example of the *so what* of a systems approach. You are asked to be responsible for the continuing education of clergy in your jurisdiction. It has been observed that many of the clergy do very little to keep their skills sharp and up to date. One approach would be to get together a committee of clergy and laity, assess the training needs of the clergy, and develop and seek funding for a program responsive to those needs. But a person or group taking a systems view is likely to pursue a different course. The view would be of the judicatory as a whole with its astounding complexity of interrelationships. The group will not look for a single cause or reason for the problem. They will tend to see the deficiency in continuing education of the clergy as deriving from several interactive sources within and outside the judicatory. They will tend to think not of a static program but in terms of the many living processes that energize the daily life of the diocese. The group will recognize that action taken to provide the desired continuing education will likely set off far-reaching and seemingly inexplicable changes in other parts of the diocese.

Thus a group taking a systems approach to the problem would probably notice that the rewards of promotion and high salary seem to bear little relation to a pastor's continuing education skills. They might notice that both ecclesiastical superiors and congregational governing boards regard with suspicion clergy who too avidly pursue a course of continuing education Some years ago I staffed such a program for a metropolitan ecumenical education agency. It so happened that all six of the clergy from one denomination were young, feisty, bright, and aggressive. Hard on the heels of the program all six men were involved in a tumultuous effort to redistribute power and open lines of two-way talk in their judicatory. Their bishop to this day has sent no more candidates to this continuing education center. The social system often exercises these powerful sanctions, which intensify the dilemma.

A group taking a systems approach would consider the course of a man's entire career. They would see the needs of a fresh young seminary graduate as contrasted to those of a man in his middle years. The uncoordinated, chaotic but numerous programs of a continuing education already available would be considered. An effort would be made to achieve comprehension and coordination with regard to career span and program availability. By pursuing these and other multiple paths the systemic problem of clergy continuing education would be attacked. Unfortunately, organizations have very few groups able to see their reality as a social system. The "add on a new program" approach is still the favorite quack medicine of the day.

A complete systems theory of organizations does not exist. The best one can say is that systems thinking has influenced the perspective from which organizations are viewed. It is as if an organization were a huge house set on a windswept cliff by the sea. Partial theories exist, such as that of role relationships, which allow one to peer into some of the windows of the house and from that view infer certain facts about the place as a whole. We know that the forces of wind and sea will eventually profoundly affect it. We know that deep within the walls are important subsystems such as plumbing and wiring. We know, moreover, that these forces and subsystems interact—but no one can as yet capture the

arrangement is a general prevalence of freedom of conscience and religious faith, and of the voluntary principle, as it is called; that is, the
promotion of every religious work by the free will offerings of the
people."[1]

Schaff traveled to America to try to understand this new nation. Like
several other such visitors, he anticipated the crucial importance of the
decision to adopt the voluntary principle in the separation of church and
state. He was intrigued with the long-range effects of leaving the church
with only a moral claim upon people's lives. After almost two hundred
years the implications are still often obscure to American church people.
This right to associate freely in a common cause is so much a part of
us that we have difficulty in recognizing the systemic influence it has had
on American church life.

Writing in 1832, the Frenchman Achille Murat emphasized the way
the voluntary principle had worked to give power to the local congregation.

Thus when a new city is founded, a lot is put aside for the first congregation
which may demand it; trustees are appointed, to whom and to their successors
in office the lands are given or sold for the use of such or such congregation.
From that moment the corporation is formed, and becomes a person empowered
to bargain and sell, to sue and be sued, according to the conditions prescribed
by the charter of incorporation. This body corporate collects gifts, borrows
money, builds a church, sells part of the pews, lets others, sells or lets choice
places in the courtyard, etc.; and when all this is done, elects a pastor, pays him,
keeps him, dismisses him, changes him, as it pleases.[2]

Not too long ago I had several phone calls from members of a troubled
congregation. They were in serious conflict with their pastor and wanted
him removed. "Can't the Bishop do something?" Like Murat a century
before, I found myself explaining to them that they were the board of
a corporation, legally chartered under the laws of the state. The bishop
had no legal power to intervene unless they gave him that power. The
law stipulates that the church board has sole authority to hire and fire
the pastor. Ecumenical and denominational cooperation between con-

gregations suffers from this reality. Competing businesses only collaborate when it is in their interest. A national drugstore chain can open and close branch stores quickly and easily in response to changing neighborhoods and market conditions. These branches are in no sense analogous to the congregations of a denominational judicatory. Each congregation must be treated as what it is: a separate legal and social entity. The power is in the people's choice of congregation to attend.

I have had some association with the ecumenical cooperative ministry planned and funded at great cost for one of our country's "new towns." The initial assumption was made that the new town dweller would not want to buy in on the competing neighborhood corner parish concept but would instead want a new, more widely cooperative and community-based form of ministry. But the observations of Murat and Schaff still hold true for even our newly planned communities. In fact, the new town citizens still preferred the local congregation to the extensively planned and funded cooperative ecumenical ministry.

The word parish in America commonly means a local congregation rather than a geographical area (its original meaning). The usage of the word reflects the fact that the associational or voluntary principle is at the heart of American church life. Clergy today still lament what they call church shopping. The expressed feeling is that people should attend the nearest congregation of their denomination. The voluntary principle has, in fact, created the local congregation on the basis of the individual's willing choice to belong and has endowed that congregation with great legal and organizational power. Modern commentators from abroad are still noting this reality.

In 1971 another Frenchman, Jean-François Revel, in his book *Without Marx or Jesus* observed that there is an indefinable religious aspect in the current ferment in American life—the Jesus movement, the practice of Zen and other Oriental religions, the general appeal of the freedom and equality of all people being outward signs of this religious aspect. Revel continues by commenting, "Above all, however, this need is being satisfied by the application of a traditional principle that has

always been successful in America; the best religions are those that you
find for yourself."[3]

Though it causes theological confusion and personal discomfort to
church leaders, the voluntary principle is a major system dynamic for the
church. It is one of the central forces that make us what we are. We
are a nation of church shoppers on the congregational level. This is why
a concern for the church in America must focus on the local parish. It
is also one of the reasons why the reform and renewal of the congregation is so difficult. The local congregation is an autonomous entity,
deriving its power from the freely chosen identification its members
have decided to make with this small outpost of the larger institution.

Finally, it is important to note that the associational principle is a way
of resolving the tension between church and culture, religion and the
state. De Tocqueville commented in 1835 that clergy "made it the pride
of their profession to abstain from politics."[4] John F. Kennedy commented often during the controversy over the possibility of a Roman
Catholic president that his private religion made no difference in his
political life. An Austrian, Francis Grund, wrote in 1837, "The Ameri-
cans consider their ministers as public servants, paid by their respective
congregations in proportion to the degree of their usefulness."[5] These
commentators were noticing the entrepreneurial basis of the American
church, each congregation, whatever the denomination, competing for
members, with clergy paid on the basis of their ability to attract them.
They were noticing that clerical blandness, public indifference, and
congregational homogeneity were possible outcomes of a nation's neutral stance toward religion. What they were observing analytically is the
vital nature of the voluntary principle as a system interface between the
institutional church and American culture. It is a system characteristic
responsible for many of our problems and much of our vitality. In the
best or the worst of American tradition the church is competing in a
buyer's market. Clerical competition, the cultural captivity of the
church, and the ill-conceived separation of religion from life find their
source to some extent in this force. At the same time, in the metropolitan area where I live there is an astonishing freedom of choice in church

membership. In a time of monstrous organizations and individual anonymity the importance of our freedom to associate in the pursuit of common beliefs is precious.

The church is an organization internally energized and structured by the voluntary principle. The freedom to elect the local congregation of one's choice is also one of the essential dynamics by which the church relates as an open system to the culture. It is the dynamic that makes the parish or congregation the leading or most influential subsystem within the church.

2. *The Symbiotic Nature of the Church*

Theorists have attempted to discern general classes or types of organization. They may be divided into profit and nonprofit categories. One such typology has been furnished by Messrs. Blau and Scott, whose classification is interesting in being based on who gains most because the organization exists.[6] They suggst four basic categories:

1. Rank-and-file members
2. The entrepreneur or manager
3. The customer or client
4. The general public

Thus if the primary beneficiary is the rank-and-file membership, then the organization fits in category 1 as a mutual benefit association. A business concern is the obvious example of category 2. Service agencies such as hospitals and social welfare organizations are examples of the third class, and finally, law enforcement agencies and state government are examples of type 4.

Where do you place the church? Is it more like a labor union or a hospital? Is a clergyman analogous to a labor leader—lifted from the membership to receive special training in leading the rank and file to attain their collective goals? Or is he more like a medical man—a trained individual who builds a "practice" based on his skill and competence in healing the spirit of the customer or client?

When I first read this typology I realized with sudden clarity that I had emerged from seminary understanding the church as a mutual benefit association. My image of my own role was accordingly far closer to that of the labor leader than the doctor. I saw myself as called to help lead a band of militant, excited Chritians on a mission in the world. I scorned the gas-station image of the congregation as a place where people went to get their tank filled when they got spiritually empty; I was so caught up in what I thought the church *ought* to be that I could not let myself see what it really is. This personal note is not just an example of the need to have a clear view of the institution. It illustrates more profoundly the enormous difficulty of rational thought about symbolic concerns. For several years my wishes for myself and the church stood in the way of my seeing the side of the institution that makes it a service organization. People turn to the church because they are looking for new life. At birth and at death, in loneliness or frenzy, people ask to be healed. I am confident that it is this search for regeneration touching the deepest elements of man's spirit that leads people to commit themselves to the church. They come primarily not to join but to be healed. I believe the church is correctly placed as a service organization, though it must be noted that the service church members expect from it is hard to measure. It is intrinsic—highly symbolic, often mysterious—with multiple psychological dimensions.

The glue that gives any organization its firmness and shape is psychological. A social system is a matrix held together by human attitudes, emotions, and values. Some theorists talk of sociotechnical systems, having noticed that the technology of an organization affects the living system. The research department has trouble with the production department not just because their goals are different, but because of differences in both technology and people. Difficulties in integrating the two departments stem from both technology and psychology. The technology the church is engaged in is spiritual renewal. The fact that this is our technology is functionally crucial. The service or technology we have to offer—such as liturgical worship—is highly symbolic, potentially touching the deepest reaches of man's being.

Katz and Kahn point out that organizations differ importantly in the degree to which their integration is biologically based, or is on the other hand a social fabrication.[7] The distinction rests on the extent to which the social patterns of the organization are symbiotically derived from early family experience or arise from the social and technological demands of the various etablished organizational roles and positions. Symbiosis implies that the patterns and forms of integration in the organization reflect those of family life. Herein lies the uniqueness of the church as a social system: It is the institution in society that goes furthest toward being an organizational incarnation of man's deepest dilemmas. Both theologically and scripturally, the church has always seen the orders of ministry, worship, and sacrament as being rooted in the transcendent. The noun *order* is a peculiarly ecclesiastical word in our language because of its common and ancient use in the church. To order means to arrange, systematize, or organize. The church has claimed—and I am certain it is functionally true—that our organization is fundamentally related to the ultimate dimensions of life—to the revealed truth of what man is meant to be. Our discipline, ritual, and order are organizational forms conformed to man's search for his destiny. These orders deeply and symbolically reflect the developmental issues with which a person begins to struggle from the moment of his emergnce from the womb. On the level of the individual and his relation to the institution examples abound.

I once worked for some time with a pastor and through him with his governing board on an initial problem presented as "reorganizing the vestry." The pastor believed he was ordained to be the chief pastor of his flock and that the structure of the church board needed to reflect that reality. I noticed that although this man seldom stated his own position clearly, he was often angry when lay people took an initiative which went against his unstated wishes. He saw his intended organization of the congregation and governing board as a way of ensuring that his ordained authority would not be circumvented. Eventually, through organization consultation and individual psychotherapy, the pastor's perception changed. He came to see the effects of his own leadership style and the roots of that style in his early relationship with his father. His desire was for the church to be an ideal family uncontaminated by the unresolved psychic struggles of his childhood. Yet he came to see the connections between his own search for identity, his theological view of the parish, and his urge to structure the congregation. On the basis of an extensive psychotherapeutic practice with clergy, Dr. Margaretta Bowers has dramatically demonstrated the commonplace existence of this same symbolic and psychodynamic parallel between the theology and ritual of the church and the individual clergyman's quest for self-hood.[8] The point is that few people expect their business organization to reflect patterns of ideal family life.

Erik Erikson suggests that organized religion is "the institution which tries to give dogmatic permanence to a reaffirmation of that basic trust and a renewed victory over that basic mistrust—with which each human being emerges from early infancy."[9] Erikson is giving positive expression to the fact that people seek an answer in the church to life's earliest and deepest dilemmas, and that the orders and forms of the church are responses shaped to these needs.

It was Freud who first helped us to see the bridge between the stuff of myth, symbol, and dream and the everyday behavior of a human being. My dreams are windows onto the dilemmas of my daily life, which in turn have their genesis in my history as a human being. This is called primary process thinking. Erikson is pointing to the link between the inner reality of primary process and the organized, orderly patterns of that social system, the church. A cathedral is an incarnate dream capturing in stone and stained glass man's hope for an eternal trusting relationship with his ultimate Creator. Baptism is a symbolic rebirth into a family which promises always to extend trust and forgiveness.

All organizations reflect to some degree a pattern of social integration based on symbiotic, primary process issues. To some degree the pattern of authority relationships will be reflective of the collective resolution of the father-son dilemma of early childhood. In most organizations these relationships are almost impossible to discern except in cases of individual pathology. I suggest that the church is unique in its two-thousand-year-old provision of an order of things fashioned toward realization of man's destiny of reintegration with ultimate Authority. Whether it is the right order of things is a matter each man must decide. I shall return to that question many times in this book. At this point I am setting forth a reality for study. The behavioral scientist must examine it for what he can learn in the exaggerated and wondrous example of the church.

3. The Ideological System

Roger Harrison, a social psychologist, has suggested that one means of looking into an organization is in terms of its ideological orientation as a system. By ideology is meant the systems of thought by which people make sense of it.[10] The ideology functions to give people cognitive maps by which they make their way in the system, and it also provides a justification for the way the organization treats people and relates to the environment. Every organization has an ideology. It derives from both pragmatic, factual values and transcendent, symbolic beliefs. The church differs only in that our ideology is both product and process. We offer a theology to members as well as having, like all organizations, an ideological system which shapes the processes of organizational life. We agree to furnish to our members cognitive maps by which people can make their way in the world, not just in the church. Every organization has a set of values which shape the kinds of behavior sanctioned by the system; they influence the role expectations and pressures that prevail and help to specify the nature of legitimate interaction by the organization with the environment. The church not only has such a system but tries, as a service product, to provide a universal value system for its members. As folk wisdom has it: Practice what you preach. The use of churchly language to say that it is important to harmonize what you do with what you advise others to do is not accidental. It reflects the fact that the church is in business to preach—to set forth a road map for life. Most organizations are not forced to be articulate about their ideology as often as the church. On the other hand I believe every institution is judged at some level on whether or not it practices what it preaches.

That judgment in the case of the church was illustrated for me by a woman who was describing her reasons for dropping out of the life and activity of a congregation. She said that she knew the church proclaimed love and forgiveness, but that every time she went to a congregational activity she found the members engaging in such petty gossip and backbiting comment about the pastor that she finally decided to quit. In her words, "No one really cared enough to talk to him."

Let us look more carefully at the ideological system of an organization. Remember that it is only one window—one facet of a social system. Example: a small congregational preschool for forty children from three to five years of age.

The preschool believes in cooperative interaction with parents and a free, lively, exploratory environment for the children. These values have led to the structuring of a parent cooperative role in the daily life of the school. The values are also reflected in sanctions concerning the role behaviors of both teachers and mother helpers. The word norm is used to refer to behaviors seen as appropriate or required modes of conduct for members of an organization. Like most organizational norms, these favored ways of behaving have never been articulated by the school. The role behavior of teachers and parental assistants is shaped by organizational pressures as subtle as a frown or as direct as an appointment to the board of the school. If a mother in her helper role carefully lines the children up in simple file to march up the hill to the playground, there is no doubt she will soon learn that things are not done that way in this school. The teacher may say something to her directly, or the mother may simply notice the difference in the way other groups of children are moving about with happy confusion.

In interviewing applicants for a vacancy on the teaching staff the ideological system is operative in shaping the qualities sought in the new teacher. The interview committee is specifically looking for a person who can work well with the parents and enjoys a free, open classroom situation with the children.

The school's ideological system cannot operate in closed isolation from the cultural values of the community or the individual sets of values brought by each member of the school. One point of this interface is quite apparent. There is no unifying cultural value concerning issues of freedom and structure with children. Dr. Spock, in fact, is a controversial symbol for this very reason. The school has been forced to recognize that every parent entering the school is a question mark and may or may not understand and support the ideological system of the school. A great deal of effort has gone into shaping a contract with parents so as to allow for personal family flexibility and yet make clear the importance the school gives to parental involvement. Communication with new parents is not easy, for very few assumptions can be made about the values they hold about child-rearing and their own role as parents in the school.

Thus the ideological system is the dynamic that illuminates and justifies the ways in which the school interacts with the community, the nature of its social and psychological contract with parents, and the shaping of organizational norms and role behaviors. This parish preschool is very different from another preshcool only a mile away. That school's stance in the community, toward parents, with children, and in what it looks for in its staff is quite different. The difference is best analyzed and brought to the surface by looking at each preschool through the lens of its respective ideological system. In design form, the elements of the system may be seen in the accompanying diagram.

An Organization's Ideological System

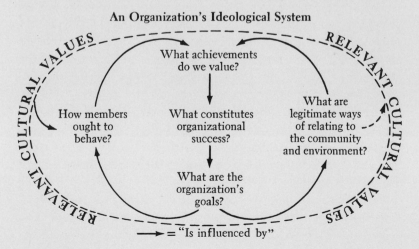

At times criticism is leveled at the organization consultant or re-searcher that he is acting as if it did not matter what people believe or where they place their values. In fact it does matter, and the real point is that there are significant connections between the values we hold and the kinds of institutions we operate. Organizations *do* have an ideology —or better, an ideological system. It is a system because all its elements operate as an interdependent whole with no single center of control. To see the whole as a system avoids the trap of simplistic logic about the organization. It is not the case that all one has to do to understand an organization is to know the values held by its leadership. This ignores the reality that their values are a part of the system—shaped by their roles, influenced by the strategies adopted by the organization, altered by changing cultural symbols.

Individual congregations within one judicatory have very different ideological systems. We see one congregation turning over its property to the community around it because they so highly value their identifica-tion with the neighborhood. Nearby in the same judicatory another moves to the suburbs and sues those who remain behind to claim a legacy left to the original parish.

Congregational or parish affiliation within a denomination reminds me of an alliance of independent grocers. Even in the most bishop-centered denominations the relationship with the judicatory and large denomination has been based on symbolic values and a wish to receive certain goods and services in return for the alliance. It must never be forgotten that the bulk of financial and psychological power is at the local level. When we look at the ideological system it is important to notice that our culture contains conflicting religious myths and symbols. The difference between the extremes of the systemic value structure of congregations has grown tremendously. This has brought a real weaken-ing of the symbolic ties with the denominations. It has been my experi-ence that to people on both left and right, their local parish has seemed like a solitary ideological refuge in a denomination filled with drift and discord.

Practice what you preach is a maxim as applicable to institutions as to the preacher. Organizations preach by their choices of goals, strategies, rewards, incentives, and members fully as clearly as the man in a pulpit.

SUMMARY

People turn to the church to receive a service. The nature of that service is daringly intangible. It is most certainly grounded in the issues of trust, self-acceptance, and identity first encountered in the relationship between child and parent. These are simply psychological ways of expressing the biblical promise of new being which is the gift of faith. The church both teaches and embodies a set of values in its organizational life. The degree of congruence between what we say and do is crucial if people are to find truth voluntarily rather than from authority pure and simple. In a sense every institution in our society must now prove itself, as people increasingly measure for themselves the reality of what they experience beside the message the organization has proclaimed.

1. Quoted in Milton Powell, ed., *The Voluntary Church* (New York: The Macmillan, Co., 1967), pp. 143, 147.

2. Quoted ibid., pp. 51–52.

3. Jean-François Revel, *Without Marx or Jesus* (Garden City, N.Y.: Doubleday, Co., 1971), p. 217.

4. Quoted in Powell, ed., op. cit., p. 90.

5. Quoted ibid., p. 78.

6. Peter M. Blau and W. Richard Scott, *Formal Organizations: A Comparative Approach* (San Francisco: Chandler Publishing Co., 1962), pp. 42–45.

7. D. Katz and R. L. Kahn, *The Social Psychology of Organizations* (New York: John Wiley & Sons, 1966), pp. 34–35.

8. Margaretta K. Bowers, *Conflicts of the Clergy* (New York: Thomas Nelson, 1964).

9. Erik Erikson, *Young Man Luther* (New York: W. W. Norton & Co., 1958), p. 257.

10. Roger Harrison, "Understanding Your Organization's Character," *Harvard Business Review* (May-June 1972), 119–28.

3

Leadership and Power

The congregation had been under grievous strain. Only three months earlier a manifesto had been presented to the clergy and governing board condemning a number of actions of the clergy. One signer said he had left the parish and was going elsewhere—"to a congregation—not a minister-run church." Another said that the rector had just not provided the necessary leadership. Other voices were raised, but the issue of leadership was a central complaint of the forty disenchanted backers of the manifesto. The governing board had asserted leadership of their own and refused to allow the conflict to be seen or handled as simply an issue between the clergy and the dissident group. One layman had said, It is our job to cope with this. The rector was persuaded not to send a letter he had prepared to the congregation—a letter which enunciated his traditional and legal authority to take some of the actions which were part of the controversy. A planning committee of the board suggested a weekend of work for the group to explore leadership, to discover where it was lacking and to define areas of responsibility. As the weekend progressed it became evident that part of what was being called the leadership problem was in fact a mixed, ambiguous set of expectations for the roles of the clergy. Areas of responsibility between the clergy and the church board were clarified. One man said it was the first time the clergy had stated clearly and openly how they view their roles. The thorny problem remained the question of leadership. Many of the board's expectations of the rector were actually their prescriptions for an effective style of leadership. They said he should:

> —Act with force but diplomacy.
> —Instruct, advise, direct, coordinate, and
> evaluate staff and lay leaders.
> —Utilize people resources—ask, tell, cajole.
> —Exhibit a genuine concern for all parishioners,
> and go more than halfway.

The church board was seeking as hard and honestly as it could to instruct its clergy in a more effective leadership style. The charged atmosphere and actual behavior indicated little movement. On Sunday morning the break-through occurred. Two consultants had been working with the group throughout the weekend. One had presented a theory on style of leadership, using as theoretical model an article from the *Harvard Business Review* by Robert Tannenbaum and Warren Schmidt.[1]

The model describes a variety of styles of leadership, defined as to the use of authority by the leader. At the far left of the diagram the leader simply tells the group what he is going to do. At the far right, he has no more authority than any other member of the group and is committed to going along with whatever the group decides.

The consultant, using actual examples from the weekend, demon-

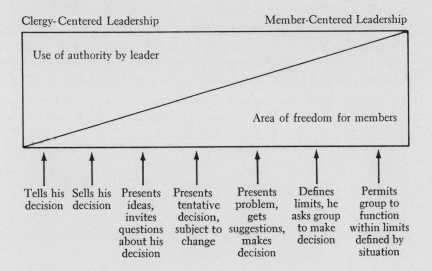

Clergy-Centered Leadership   Member-Centered Leadership

Use of authority by leader

Area of freedom for members

| Tells his decision | Sells his decision | Presents ideas, invites questions about his decision | Presents tentative decision, subject to change | Presents problem, gets suggestions, makes decision | Defines limits, he asks group to make decision | Permits group to function within limits defined by situation |

strated by this theory the way in which the rector's leadership rapidly ranged from autocratic to permissive laissez faire. The clergyman felt he was acting in a participative manner toward the church board, which in turn felt the rector's approach to be a disguised autocracy, and that he gave them little freedom to decide significant church issues. Through the help of the consultants the board was enabled to understand its bewilderment and frustration with the rector's leadership. The rector was helped to see that he was using different styles of leadership in a random, chaotic fashion. These insights were new to him. The purpose of the theory was to help him see where his leadership style was appropriate and where it needed to be adjusted; the theory was a framework for aiding the leader to perceive leadership situations more clearly and hence to respond appropriately. In this case the church board could never be sure whether the rector was telling them, consulting them, or asking them to take initiative and move ahead, deciding their own

directions. Depending on circumstances, any one stance if made explicit
might be appropriate. But proffered in a haphazard, distorted, unknow-
ing fashion, it resulted in confusion, suspicion, and a growing lack of
trust between leader and member. By being given a way to understand
their dilemma, clergy and laity took the first small step toward coping
with the congregation and its problems.

THE NATURE OF LEADERSHIP

The search for effective leaders haunts every institution. Writing in
Harper's Magazine, Col. David Hackworth bemoans the confusion in
the Army between genuine leaders of men and staff technologists.[2]
Philosophers have debated for centuries the question of whether the
charismatic leader changes history, or the times evoke the man to meet
the situation. Who is a leader, and what is this thing called leadership?
The two questions imply that leadership is both a process and a role or
status grouping. Leadership refers both to something you are and something you do. The clergy are leaders by virtue of their status. But what
is it a leader does—what is the process of leadership?

Leadership is "interpersonal influence, exercised in situations and
directed, through the communication process, toward the attainment of
a specified goal or goals. Leadership always invokes attempts on the part
of a leader (influencer) to affect (influence) the behavior of a follower
(influencee) or followers in the situation."[3] The church board's advice
to the rector to "act with force but diplomacy" was their prescription
to him on how to increase his positive influence with members. At that
point the board was assuming leadership toward the rector. It was trying
to influence his behavior.

Recall that the church is a widely scattered institution. Its front line
is the local congregation. The voluntary nature of the American church
dictates that this is the level at which people turn over their money and
psychic energy for the empowerment of the church. When the church
starts up a new congregation, the first thing it does is to hire a clergyman.
His job is to influence a group of people to join together in common to

become a worshiping, teaching, serving fellowship. From beginning to end the pivotal leader in the congregation is the clergyman. In the files of Project Test Pattern and in my own experience, I have found time and again that the rector's leadership is the crucial dimension of congregational life. It has been shown that the designated leader of a group is the primary keeper of the organization's norms. That is, he has most power to change the prescribed and accepted ways of behaving in the system. At the same time, the leader is also the person most influenced by—most conforming to—the norms of the organization. The leader is both keeper of, and kept by, the culture of his organization. The rector in the instance recounted above was the person most responsible for the climate of mistrust and suspicion. He was also the person most influenced by the resultant hostility and lack of candor. As the case demonstrates, the influence of lay leadership is the foundation for an effective clergy. By aggressively taking the congregational conflict as their own problem, by candor in their dealing with the clergy, these lay leaders saved the day.

This functioning concept of shared leadership is a practical necessity for a vital institution. It is important not to equate shared leadership with never taking the initiative or with a laissez-faire style on the part of the designated leader. Shared leadership does not mean giving up power so as to become weak or helpless. What it does mean is that leadership functions (which may often be initiating—i.e., telling or directing actions) are appropriately shared among the people involved in the organization. The effective leader has the capacity to diagnose a situation so as to read accurately what functions are needed by the group in relation to the task to be performed. There has been a tendency in behavioral science literature to search for an ideal leadership style on some kind of continuum between attention to people and attention to task. Much useful discussion has arisen from this search, but increasingly the facts seem to show that the effectiveness of an over-all leadership style or of acts of leadership by individuals is highly situational. Some tasks call for group discussion, consensual decision-making, and a democratic, people-oriented style of leadership. Other tasks and situations

need unilateral action on the part of the designated leader, telling people
what to do. The effective leader (and it may be any member of the
group) is a diagnostician who can modify his role and function according
to the needs of the members and the task of the group. The clergyman
who really understands and makes good use of the concept of shared
leadership actually gains power. People regard him as a strong enabler
—a person of authority who uses it appropriately to get the job done,
allowing room for others to make their contribution. He is a person who
knows, in his dealings with others, the significance of the self.

It is easy for the church to misunderstand the nature of the leadership
process at the local church level. Here is a contrasting example: two
clergy, in similar socioeconomic situations—each with an affluent, hard-
driving, family-oriented congregation. Both men wish to lead their congregations toward a greater social commitment and deeper understanding of the Christian faith. Pastor A is unstinting in his labors. He is
always on call—involved in liberal causes in the community, never too
busy to see church members, counsels heavily. He is concerned with the
lack of commitment in the congregation and has trouble getting sus-
tained attendance at the educational programs he has launched. However, he is well loved in the church. People praise his devotion and say
they are glad he is involved even though they do not always support his
stands.

Pastor B works hard, but also takes time off for himself and his family.
He limits his parish and community involvement. He is less concerned
with lack of commitment in the congregation, and in fact can speak with
deep empathy of the pressures upon the family life of members. He has
been meeting quietly for some months with a group of businessmen in
the congregation—enormously talented and powerful men. The group
has helped each man to identify some of the personal talents he had to
contribute and to think through some ways in which they could be used
in the community. Several of the men have become involved; one
recently assisted an agency in the community to obtain a federal grant
of several hundred thousand dollars for a new assistance program.

Both Pastor A and Pastor B are well liked. Neither congregation is in serious trouble. The two men have similar goals. Leadership is the pastor's attempt to influence the members toward the attainment of these goals. In this light the effective leader is apparent. By the legitimizing power of their office the men are equal; the influence they are able to exert toward the desired goals is quite different.

I hope it is becoming apparent that to poke our nose into leadership it is necessary to think once again in systems terms. To examine leadership means to look beyond the individual leader to the whole system by which power, authority, and influence are exercised in the organization. Recall again the Tannenbaum theory used at the church board weekend conference described earlier: the basic ingredient in that model was the degree to which the designated leader used the power ascribed to him. Some members of that congregation saw the clergy as exercising power in an arbitrary and capricious way. The point of clarification for the clergy came when they realized that they were using power inconsistently, unconsciously, and inappropriately.

LEADERSHIP POWER

Leaders receive power (actual potential to influence others) from several sources. The nature of power and its distribution is one of the distinguishing characteristics of the church. It is one of the best ways to understand what is happening and why.

Officials or formal leaders receive some of their power by the authority of their office. Board members receive legal authority because they are officers of a corporation chartered under the laws of the state. Some positions carry with them the power to impose physical sanctions ("put that foul-up on KP duty") or provide material rewards ("I think Johnson deserves a raise"). Power of these two kinds is not limited to designated authorities, as witness the effectiveness of an individual who provides the chief financial support to a voluntary organization. Power that derives from the capacity to coerce physically or offer practical rewards obviously is not limited to persons designated by traditional or legal authority.

Aside from personal status, authority also flows from the tradition of the institution. The chief pastor of a congregation has power because people expect it of him. As one vestry said to their rector, "We expect you to be in charge at all times." The great social theorist Max Weber said that the ultimate source of this traditional authority is the charisma of the original leaders.[4] He pointed out that the more the authority of an office depends on charismatic elements the greater the crisis of succession. The aptness of his thought is evident when one watches a congregation struggling to choose a new minister. It usually takes only a week or so before someone notices aloud that "we seem to be searching for a combination of St. Paul and Jesus." Charismatic authority is really a kind of personal power, attached to the formal office by way of traditional linkage with charismatic figures in the organization. The doctrine of apostolic succession implies that a priest has personal power due to the unbroken chain of ordination back to the original apostles.

Both formal and informal leaders have personal power other than that derived from legitimate authority. In today's complex world expert knowledge can bring power. It may also come from having access to key persons and resources. It may come from providing vital linkage between people who need to work and talk together. Much of whatever strength I have within my own organization comes from such sources. I have some knowledge of education, training, and organizational life, and easy access to the Bishop and other key persons; I also serve as a link between various groups and organizations. This linking role gives me a certain power with each group for which I provide this vital function.

In addition, both formal and informal leaders have influence over others based upon the affection and respect with which they are regarded. This power derives from the relationship and is related to control based on rewards of acceptance, esteem, and love. There are certain people and groups whose respect and esteem I value enough so that they may influence my actions; I am more vulnerable or open to influence by some persons and groups than others. The pastor of the parish I attended as an adolescent exercised great influence on my life because of my own deep intrapsychic needs and identification with him. Today

I still respect him, but my needs are different and he no longer has the same influence. A group of professional colleagues which meets regularly in my office has power over me because I value their esteem and acceptance. They also have power because of their expert knowledge, their access to key people in the metropolitan area, and their capacity to link various judicatory programs. When Pastor B in the instance given earlier formed a peer group of wealthy businessmen, he was using these aspects of influence in order to assert leadership.

In other words, both individual and social psychological forces contribute to patterns of power based on other than physical or material reward. In particular, areas of power are likely to be found in (a) the need for expertize, (b) the necessity of linking people and groups, (c) sources of access to other power centers, and (d) personal needs for acceptance and friendship.

POWER IN THE CHURCH

Amitai Etzioni characterizes organizations that rely on control via physical sanctions as coercive-power-oriented, and those that rely on material rewards as utilitarian-power-based. Institutions that rely on control through charisma, symbolic reward (election to the governing board), esteem, acceptance, peer approval, or a high degree of personal identification with the leadership he characterizes as normative-power-oriented.[5] The church is probably the outstanding example of an institution relying primarily on normative power.

Several important facts flow from this reality. First, charisma cannot be institutionalized. Personally attractive, life-filled and life-giving people are not so easy to come by as are technically proficient, professionally trained replacements for the correct slot in the organization chart. The argument over whether clergy are professionals or not hinges on this point. Part of what a congregational pastor needs to be—a person with whom others can identify and toward whom they have positive feelings of affection and trust—exceeds the customary boundaries of professional competence.

Second, the sources of power for the church are increasingly limited. There seems to be a growing trend in society to limit the areas in which the authority of institutions will be accepted. My oldest son questions the authority of his teachers in ways that never entered my mind. The area in which he is willing to suspend his own judgment and accept theirs is much narrower than was mine at his age. The rector in the conflict-laden congregation cited at the beginning of this chapter was going to send a letter to the congregation citing his traditional and legal authority. A similar letter from a different congregation and different minister but inspired by the same causes, arrived in the mail as I wrote this chapter. What both clergy fail to recognize is that the people to whom they address these letters are not willing to suspend their own judgment in favor of the invoked authority. The citing of formal authority works as an influence effort—as effective leadership—only when the follower is willing to accept it.

Daniel Katz has emphasized that it is in the very nature of our culture to justify our role in an organization by the need for that role in effective operation of the organization rather than by tradition or moral correctness. He postulates three kinds of belonging to an organization—symbolic, normative, and instrumental.[6]

Symbolic attachment refers to "emotionally held attitudes in which the symbols [i.e., the flag] represent absolute values and have a life of their own."

Normative involvement is "the acceptance of specific legitimate requirements of the system necessary for system membership" (for the organization to work well I must live by its norms, i.e., approved ways of behaving).

Functional involvement has to do with "commitment to the system because its demands are instrumental to his needs" (physical, material, and spiritual needs).

The trend toward membership based on functional and normative vs. less symbolic involvement is a movement toward greater reliance on personal choice and away from the forces of tradition. Much of the traditional authority of the church has derived from the power of symbolic involvement. The right to excommunicate derives its strength from the symbolic power of the Eucharist. A clergyman has had rights and functions by virtue of the strength of the symbol of ordination. If Katz is correct—and I believe he is—symbolic involvement in our institutions is giving way in importance to a commitment based directly on functional interdependence. If I belong to your organization I will accept your standards of membership—the nature and degree of commitment desired—provided you can show me that they are necessary for the organization to be effective, and provided that membership gives me the rewards I am seeking. At first glance I think it can be argued that there is a countervailing tendency in our society. In all its aspects (Women's Lib, the youth movement, the Jesus movement, the black revolution), there is a great emphasis on symbolic belonging. The importance here is that the movement as a whole is anti-institutional and toward power distribution or equalization. Symbols and symbolic belonging have great power—but it is not readily available at this moment in history to our major institutions.

The result is simply to reinforce the fundamental point that our institutions are laboring under a tremendous erosion of their traditional sources of power. In short, every institution is having to rely more and more on controls based on a normative and functional source—the position the church in its essential nature has found to be its most potent source of strength. This is power based on positive, fulfilling human relationships, the realization of personal goals and values, the functional realities of getting the job done well and creatively. A power dependent more on personal and group attributes than on canon law or tables of organization is what leaders are turning to for the influence needed to exercise effective leadership.

Thus far I have spoken of leadership and not management. The words are often synonymous. Management usually includes a broad range of functions, such as planning, organizing, and administering, which are not a part of leadership. The latter is a concept more narrowly confined to human factors of influencing others to achieve desired ends. All good managers are leaders, but all leaders do not need to be managers. The less traditional or legal authority a manager has, the more he must work at being a good leader. The shift I have described in sources of power in an organization, and the coupled necessity for an emphasis on the manager being a leader, form one way of describing a major thrust in management theory in recent years. Douglas McGregor, the late Sloan Professor of Management at MIT, is often cited as a founder of this movement. McGregor saw clearly that for too long management had operated on a mechanical-rational understanding of man, which led in turn to organizations built solely on extrinsic systems of control, reward, and punishment. He regarded the emphasis on coercive and utilitarian power as deriving from a false view of man: that people have to be pushed, shoved, or led to get anything done—the philosophy of the carrot and the stick. McGregor took another look and decided that human beings were also thinking, feeling, loving, questing mortals, each with his own goals and values. In taking this more accurate organic view of man he was able to say that *"the most appropriate managerial strategy, according to this theory, is to create an organizational environment in which man perceives the most attractive opportunities for achieving his dominant goals to lie in expending effort toward organizational goals."*[7][italics mine]

McGregor believed that apathy and hostility toward an organization's goals were symptoms of the fact that "the organizational environment is not perceived to offer the best opportunities for achieving [the individual's] goals that are dominant."[8] In speaking of an individual's aims and purposes he did not confine himself to such extrinsic rewards as money, praise, social acceptance, or recognition. He was perhaps even more concerned with the intrinsic rewards relating to such things as self-achievement, altruism, the giving of love and help, and the creative solution of a difficult problem. By recognizing that man is by nature striving to satisfy a wide range of needs, through both extrinsic and intrinsic rewards, McGregor is saying that among the alternatives available to him, an individual will choose those situations which appear to be best for the achievement of his goals. And he is suggesting leadership based on power derived from the members rather than imposed by the leaders.

His insight was beautifully illustrated for me at a recent dinner party my wife and I attended. The two other couples present were Peace Corps volunteers and perfect examples of the young generation which is turned off by the church. The evening was an exciting blend of honest, caring debate and wide-ranging discussion of religion, the search for self, parenthood, parents, and the norms of American and foreign cultures. As the evening was drawing to a close one of the men turned to me and said, "You know, Jim, if I believed that on some regular basis I could meet with a group like this I would love to do it once a week or so—not only that—I would even be happy to call that experience 'church.' "

For this bright young man, as for so many others with whom I have talked, his acquaintance with the church has taught him that the best opportunities for achieving his goals are not to be found there.

As his final charge to the apostle upon whom the church was to be founded, Jesus said to Peter, "Feed my sheep" (John 21:17). In consulting with congregations over problems of withdrawal, conflict, and lack of vitality, I have discovered the power of this biblical concept to expose the very problem that Douglas McGregor has so clearly delineated. In a congregation racked by intense conflict one man actually put it this way: "When I come here on Sunday morning the worship no longer feeds me. I find I get more of what I need for my spirit some days when I am here during the week and go and sit in the church alone. Moreover, I believe this is the key. That is, if we had been providing more feeding experiences, more experiences where people could get something of what they are after out of church, we would never have had so much trouble."

I believe this man accurately points up the fact that much of the frustration present in his congregation has arisen out of their inability to provide experiences which in some measure satisfy the needs of members. Like my Peace Corps friends, he is speaking of the kinds of services he would like from the church, and of the power the church might have in his life it it were really to provide those services. The working committee of which this man is a part has adopted as a banner over their work the slogan of "providing more feeding experiences for the people of this parish."

A primary task of leadership is to create situations in which the attainment of individual goals can be seen and experienced in the achievement of the organization's goals. "*What leadership does is enable the individual to satisfy his psychological needs by his own actions, which are the very actions sought by the leader to achieve the purpose of the organization* [italics mine]."[9]

Leadership strategy is more and more influential as our institutions struggle with new forms of power and new societal values. It seems to be essential to an institution that promises new life and spiritual renewal to those who will commit themselves as faithful members.

The power of leaders and the commitment of members are like the two sides of a coin. It is possible to flip the coin into the air, see which side it lands on, and examine that side closely. But whether we are saying heads or tails, we are speaking of one coin and its value is that of the whole; head and tail are finally inseparable. Leadership and membership are two sides of the same coin. It is possible to examine them separately, but the worth of an organization lies in their relation of wholeness.

1. Robert Tannenbaum and Warren Schmidt, "How to Choose a Leadership Pattern," *Harvard Business Review* (March-April 1958), p. 96.

2. David Hackworth, "Commentary—A Soldier's Digest," *Harper's Magazine* (July 1972), pp. 74–78.

3. Robert A. Tannenbaum and Fred Masarik, "Leadership: A Frame of Reference" *Management Science,* (October 1957), p. 3. Quoted in Fremont E. Kast and James E. Rosenzweig, *Organization and Management* (New York: McGraw-Hill Book Co., 1970).

4. Max Weber, *On Charisma and Institution Building,* (Chicago: University of Chicago Press, 1968), pp. 54–61.

5. Amitai Etzioni, *Modern Organizations* (Englewood Cliffs, N. J.: Prentice-Hall, 1964), p. 59.

6. Daniel Katz, "Group Process and Social Integration," *Journal of Social Issues* (January 1967), p. 18.

7. Douglas McGregor, *The Professional Manager* (New York: McGraw Hill Book Co., 1967), pp. 136–37.

8. Ibid., p. 137.

9. Douglas S. Sherwin, "Strategy for Winning Employee Commitment," *Harvard Business Review* (May-June 1972), pp. 37–47.

4

Membership and Motivation

THE PSYCHOLOGICAL CONTRACT

The congregational newsletter proclaimed in its lead story that the church is people—people working, worshiping, entering into relationship with one another—people with mutual interests and values sharing with one another. The article added, "because it is people who enter into relationships of work and worship, I am continually perplexed by church members who rarely, if ever, participate by simply showing up."

Why don't people show up—the question recurs and echoes from the empty pews. "What do we have to do to motivate people to take part?" asked one lay woman. "Why aren't people more committed?" asks another. It may be that we are all too conditioned to the presence of mass media advertising in our daily existence. There seems to be a cultural belief that given enough money, creative thinking, and engaging eye-catching publicity, people can be motivated.

The assumption is misleading. Apathy, indifference, lack of participation, resistant behavior, all are signs that the organization is not living up to its psychological contract with its memebers. It is not paying back in proper terms for the expenditure of psychic energy, time, or money it would like to demand from the member. Every individual develops a psychological contract with the organization. Unlike a legal contract it will never be put into writing, and many of its most important elements will always be in a state of dynamic flux. Nevertheless, there exists between the individual and the organization a set of expectations—each of the other—which in fact determine organizational membership. If either party reneges on the contract then the harmonious relationship is impaired, and if this happens often the social system is in trouble.

Leadership theory says that a person's needs or motives lead him to behave in ways designed to fulfill his hoped-for rewards or goals. A task of leadership is to create conditions for the setting and support of a valid psychological contract between the individual and the organization. This should validate the attainment of the individual's goals through achievement of the organization's goals. Institutions must live within the tension of effectively responding to the purposes of their members and at the same time functioning so that the organization as a whole is thriving and carrying out its purposes.

WHY PEOPLE PARTICIPATE

Abraham Maslow has said that the needs a person brings to a situation range (in a hierarchy) from basic motivations for food, survival, and safety to the need for socialization to needs for self-esteem and self-actualization.[1] Assuming that leadership finds its power for moving the institution by responsiveness to the functional involvement of the members, it is apparent that providing food, money, and even a climate of involvement and belonging are not enough. The human quest for a sense

of self-affirmation—a sense of dignity, worth, and self-realization—is as
powerful as the need for food and safety. As a result, dissatisfaction with
one's work or organizational life is a commonplace in the American
scene. The assembly-line blue-collar worker has no monopoly on the
malaise of personal helplessness.

"The Blue-Collar Blues are prominently associated with those working conditions (without regard to income) that discourage good work
performance, impede personal growth, fail to stimulate hard and fast
work and that stifle autonomony and creativity."[2]

Over the centuries the church has provided food, shelter, and sanctuary to countless thousands. Today countless others as urgently seek a
different level of fulfillment. The need to belong, the need for self-
esteem, the need for self-actualization are hungers to which the worship
and ministry of the church are addressed.

Maslow points out the important fact that a need once met no longer
motivates. The task of staying in touch with the needs of a congregation
—understanding the fluctuating mystery of what it is they hope to give
and receive as members—is a fascinating challenge for congregational
leaders. It is also a challenge which goes against a prevailing church
norm. Church people are not "supposed" to talk about what they want
from the organization. Unselfish commitment rather than self-serving
participation is the way the norm reads. This sometimes hinders people
in speaking out regarding their own personal values and feelings, and
leads instead to generalized comment about what the church "ought"
to be or do. Yet the psychological contract between individuals and the
congreagation as a whole is extremely varied, highly intangible, difficult
to determine, and constantly changing. There is no one simple answer
as to why people do or do not take part.

Recently the leadership of a congregation had twelve refusals from
individuals approached to be nominated for election to its governing
board. Those who refused were interviewed to find out why they had
said No. The leaders assumed that the reasons for such a resounding
negative must involve disappointment or perhaps even hostility toward
some aspect of church life. In fact, this turned out to be true of only

one out of the dozen. Rather than disdain, anger, disappointment, or even indifference, these people simply had other things to do which were seen by each of them as more important, satisfying, enriching, or personally suitable. They were happy with the church, personally fond of the minister, had no intention of going elsewhere, gave money, and in most cases attended worship on a consistent basis. *The task of serving on the board of deacons did not motivate them.*

In trying to understand this information I was reminded of Frederick Herzberg's theoretical formulation concerning people's motivation to work.[3] He takes Maslow's concept of a hierarchy of needs one step further by distinguishing between motivators and demotivators. His research has shown that opportunities for personal achievement, recognition, increased responsibility, a chance for advancement, and the opportunity to grow in knowledge and competence are positive task motivators. The presence of these factors lends excitement, reward, and satisfaction to the work. Factors such as working conditions, salary, fringe benefits, the nature of supervision, company policies, and administrative procedures he found to be essentially preventive maintenance or hygienic in nature. That is, they could cause poor task motivation and were sources of dissatisfaction—but they were not, no matter how satisfactory, sources of personal satisfaction. Herzberg's theories have been extensively adapted into practice and have proved to be extremely useful.[4] His basic point is that for a task to be enriching to a participant it should be as full of the motivating factors (achievement, recognition, professional growth, and responsibility) as possible and as free of the demotivators (poor supervision, inadequate policies and administration, poor interpersonal relations, low wages or status) as possible. But merely having excellent maintenance factors will not make up for inadequate, boring tasks.

This is precisely what lay men and women were saying about the task of serving on the governing board of their congregation. They had no quarrel with their relation to the clergy on either a supervisory or an interpersonal level. They were not opposed to current church policies; no hint was given that they scorned the symbolic honor of being elected.

The fact was the task itself was not sufficiently challenging to capture their energy. If the problem of their lack of motivation is to be solved, the answer lies in redesigning the work to be done—changing the nature of the task itself. Publishing the names of the congregational board in the Sunday bulletin, improving the supervision of the clergy, overcoming hostilities to parish policy will not make up for a limiting, barely tolerable, uninteresting job to be done.

I have developed sixteen-question survey of church board work team characteristics which I use with boards to help them develop their own sense of their style of work. The individual member responds to each item by indicating how characteristic he feels the statement is of the life of the board. Two of the items are as follows:

7. We spend too much time debating issues that are relatively unimportant and very little on the things that really count.

11. Our goals as a vestry are clear to all, shared by all, and are cared about by all.

I expect from past experience that the majority of the board will find the first statement quite characteristic and the second quite uncharacteristic. My own experience is supported by research done by the Center for a Voluntary Society. They found that the majority of businessmen working in volunteer organizations feel underutilized, that their primary skills and abilities are not being tapped, and that they are being asked to work on tasks for which they have low enthusiasm.[5] When the leadership goes to work reshaping the job to be done, it is my experience that board apathy disappears.

To create engaging, rewarding tasks is, however, no panacea. A small city congregation was concerned to have a broader-based, educationally sound, financially rewarding stewardship campaign. The governing board, acting with the advice and consent of the pastor, engaged the services of an educational specialist and a management consultant to assist with the stewardship effort. A careful scheme of education and training was devised. A series of home meetings was arranged. The whole campaign was headed by two enthusiastic lay people in the congregation. Both were relative newcomers to town and were eager to be involved and to help the campaign to be a success. The campaign was not successful. Several of the house meetings were almost deserted. Sixty people invited, forty acceptances, three showed. The level of financial giving remained static. One of the few well-attended house meetings was held at the home of one of the community's most influential citizens and a key power figure in the church. A long-time citizen of the town, this gentleman headed the financial canvass held the following year. With little organization and a narrow base of participation, it was a resounding financial success. Looking back on this experience, one of the persons who had led the first year's unsuccessful effort expressed her motivation for taking part. She said that as a newcomer she wanted to be known and to know others. She had hoped to become a part of things —in the congregation and in the community. She said she still felt closed out and was determined to keep working to broaden the base of participation. The powerful gentleman who had headed the second year's effort commented on the unsuccessful first year by saying he had been willing to give it a try but could not see the reason for so many mettings and so much time wasted. "The main thing I want from the church is the Holy Communion on Sunday morning and that's all."

This vignette illustrates the necessity of a proper appreciation by church leadership of the system of power and influence in the congregation and the widely differing needs which individuals bring to their congregational participation. Leadership involves the use of power, but in this case the leaders did not use their powerful people effectively and gained little from the membership as a whole. An engaging enterprise coupled with methods involving participation is no cure-all. In particular, the idea of fostering member motivation by a heavy emphasis on increased participation in the decision-making, program development process is an overutilized, overgeneralized approach that often fails. Participation to be of value must be at a level which picks up issues of genuine concern to the participant.[6] Giving people information and asking them to participate on behalf of matters far removed from their personal concerns can actually create problems and spread confusion. The influential businessman in the preceding example participated in the first year's stewardship effort out of pure loyalty to the congregation. His heart was not in the effort, since his need to belong, to be influential, to associate with other members of the congregation was minimal. The leadership was too quick to take the woman's need for prominent belonging as being generally true of the congregation. This could be a capsule summary of the failure of widespread use of participative planning techniques in the church. For a while it was the "in thing" to have a congregation planning for its future—aiming for change through ever wider bases of participation. A great many of these efforts failed. They failed because people participated out of duty and loyalty, but with no personal stake in the changes that might eventuate. Participation in and of itself is no guarantee of commitment. Once again, the key is to understand the source of people's commitment.

FORMS OF INVOLVEMENT

One intriguing effort to understand the different bases for organizational commitment and relation to the task to be done is embodied in the work of Thomas Bier at Case Western Reserve University. Bier describes three fundamental orientations toward an organization:

Formal——A person who enjoys direction, guidelines, recognizes formal lines of authority.

Social——A person who enjoys committee work, likes to proceed on the basis of discussion and agreement. Works toward consensus and mutual goals.

Personal——You do your thing and I'll do mine kind of person. Prime value is on being oneself.[7]

The person with a formal orientation is at home in the traditional bureaucratic organization with structured, well-defined tasks. The one with a social orientation is more comfortable with complex tasks whose shape continually changes as the result of interaction, collaboration, and consensus. An individual with a personal orientation may have difficulty functioning in any type of organizational setting. The social orientation has been an emerging life-style for the last two decades. In that period, the church has shed many of its formal, bureaucratic tendencies and has come to operate much more on the basis of mutualism, shared goals, and tasks defined in collaboration. A third possible form of organization is connective or coordinating in style. Swtichboarding—making connections so that people are helped to do their thing (and if by chance it is congruent with someone else's thing so much the better)—is the name of the game in this style of organization. Bier's work has helped me see that congregations do indeed contain people with all three orientations. The person with a formal attitude toward the organization is often quite uncomfortable and unhappy with a consensual approach. Research by the Center for a Voluntary Society confirms this fact. They have noticed a real difference in the reaction of traditional businessmen to homogeneous, formal, well-defined volunteer agencies and to the heterogeneous, representative, communally based volunteer organizations. The heated debate, wrangling, emotionally laden atmosphere of the latter is frustrating to the person with a formal outlook. In discussing their frustrations these businessmen emphasized the difficulty they have had with the imprecise characteristics of an organization modeled along collaborative, communal lines.

"It means dealing with incapable volunteers who slow down accomplishment and can't be fired" (70 percent). "Everything moves slowly compared to business. Time is wasted" (61 percent).

"It is difficult to provide leadership for groups or committees of different kinds of people trying to work together" (54 percent)[8]

One man summed it up by saying, "As a result of my experiences, I believe in self-perpetuating boards, in benevolent dictatorships, because they don't break down the way the democratic ones do."[9] The difficulty is that the solution he proposes turns off the person with a social or communal orientation. Many of the tasks to which the church must address itself require collaboration with highly diverse interest groups. In these instances democratic procedures must be employed. The prob-

lem then is to be aware that these consensual methods are strange and
uncomfortable to persons with a formal orientation.

It may be that the personal orientation so characteristic of many
young people does not fit well in either traditional or contemporary
organizations. For this emerging group of persons the connective or
coordinating style of organization seems to fit best. One good example
of it is really an invention of the youth culture—the free university. This
is simply a setting which allows people to make an offering of their skill
or talent and gives them a way to sign up for the offerings. A course goes
when someone wants to give it and someone wants to take it. Some
congregations have moved from being predominantly bureaucratic
through an emphasis on collaboration to a style that is best described
as coordinating or connective in nature. And some are flexible enough
to use all three styles, suiting the approach to the tasks and individuals
involved.

The rector of one such congregation portrayed his experience in this
vignette. "I try to see that things happen as easily and as quickly as
possible. I believe in different strokes for different folks. If we spent our
energies trying to reach consensus on where to go there would be no
energy left, so instead we work toward each of the diverse elements in
the congregation being given support for their thing. Recently I called
on a new woman in the congregation. It developed that she was recently
divorced. She began expressing her loneliness and her wish to talk with
others in her situation. I asked if she would be willing to help in
convening such a group. She said Yes. I called another divorcee in the
parish who I thought would be willing to help and gave her some names.
These two women set to work and got a group to meet which has been
meeting weekly ever since. I think that is a more realistic way for
programs to happen in a place as diverse and mobile as ours than going
through a long planning process with a lot of vestry committees."[10]

This man is describing the sensitive ear he turns toward perceiving
the members' side of the psychological contract. He emphasizes the
energy he puts into listening for what it is people are seeking from the
congregation. He is also underlining the need to recognize the diversity

of orientation, expectations, and values people bring to their membership role. By adopting a flexible, coordinating organizational style, the parish has learned to cope with an array of differences and a high turnover in membership.

CREATING FLEXIBLE INVOLVEMENT

It is no accident that this minister chose the example of calling on a newcomer in the congregation. The moment of entering a new organization is crucial for the individual as a participating member. Recall how you felt learning the ropes for the first time in school, in the Army, in a new job. For most of us, most of the time, it has been a moment of dependence on the institution—an experience of helplessness that is now confirmed by research.[11] Every new member of every institution goes through a process of socialization in which he learns the price of membership. He learns the ideology of the social system—the values, norms, and behaviors which are deemed important by that particular organization. It is the time during which a person feels most at a disadvantage and during which the initial psychological contract is set. During the first week of my new job as director of Christian education of an Episcopal parish in Palm Beach, Florida, my wife and I were invited to dinner by one of the lay leaders in the congregation. I wore my new clerical black summer suit with clerical collar. We arrived at the dinner party, which turned out to be at a fashionable beach club. A gentle ocean breeze, graceful palm trees, and soft dance music were the atmosphere surrounding us. All others at the party, including my boss the rector, were in bright, colorful, informal sports clothes. No one said a word about my dress but I was acutely aware that the process of organizational socialization had begun. I realized that I was going to have to reexamine some of the patterns of behavior which had been valued in the high-church Anglo-Catholic situation from which I was moving. With the distance of time and experience I can also see more clearly that in microcosm the incident illustrates the basic choices an individual can make within the process of organizational socialization.[12]

Two of those choices are basically failures. They are to rebel or to conform. Conformity has been the unnoticed failing of a process which itself has been unnoticed. Most formal orientations I have experienced were indoctrinations which implicitly asked for conformity. The results of conformity are the continued reinforcement from the outset of a don't-rock-the-boat norm, the burial (on a day-to-day basis) of people's disappointments with the organization, and an absence of the creativeness that occurs when an organization is genuinely open to new thought and values. The third alternative is that the socialization process leads to a response of creative individualism. In this case the psychological contract that is formed supports the individual's right to assert his own values, to question norms, to influence the system. This means the social system must be self-aware and continually reexamining the process of organizational socialization. It must be willing to scrutinize the boundary between acceptable and unacceptable behavior with clarity, firmness, and openness.

The congregation in the example of the divorced woman, in working out its coordinating-connective organization style, has emphasized the individual's early experiences with the church. They have rightly seen that these experiences have enormous impact on a person's future relationship with it. The woman in the example learned right away that the organization was willing to work with her to create situations in which she could pursue her deep personal concerns. She learned she would neither be babied nor simply told to conform. This contrasts with a socialization practice commonly used in which the newcomer is handed an information card and asked which existing church activity he would like to join (i.e., where do you want to fit in?). Sometimes the card is accompanied by an informative pamphlet which tells the new person about the organizations he may be joining. The message consists of information about present, existing, cohesive, formal organizations, so that one can more easily pick the appropriate slot. For people with a formal orientation this can be fine and is often needed. For those with a social and/or personal orientation it can be anathema. The alternative is to work out explicit procedures for the setting of a psychological contract which allows for clarity and two-way negotiation. The visit of the pastor in the example I have been using is one step in such an explicit process. In this case the visit of the rector is always followed by a visit from one of the vestry of the church. The newcomer is also told that by becoming a member he or she will automatically go on the roster for certain parish duties, such as care of the altar or service as an usher. In addition, the person's name will go into the hat for possible service on the governing board or vestry. Each year the vestry are chosen by lot. When a person's name is drawn he is called, told of the role expectations, and asked if he is willing to serve. The acceptance rate is 99 percent. Thus the newcomer may be called on by a vestry person who has been in the congregation only a year. The newcomer's picture of this congregation as a place where his values and dreams are honored and that is open to his influence will have been reinforced once again. The individual is not being asked to fit in passively, but to join and make a difference. A psychological contract is being formed which asks for open, honest communication about an individual's needs and wants and which asks the parish to listen actively to such communication. A basis is built for future undistorted renegotiation.

Another congregation which has been the subject of a Project Test Pattern study places a similar self-conscious emphasis on this process by which organizations and individuals join up with one another. They are careful to convene new members, not just to tell them about the parish but to hear from the new people their hopes and expectations. "What in your previous parish experience did you find particularly rewarding or fulfilling that you hope to find here?" This congregation asks new members to attend its intensive and extensive inquirers' group. For many participants it is an "upending experience" which characteristically raises new religious and personal issues and is upsetting to old assumptions. This upending quality is a dynamic of initiation which organizations have used for centuries in the socialization process, similar in a sense to boot camp or the novitiate period in religious orders.[13] The point is that it is done in this congregation in a deliberate, explicit manner to assist members to develop clear religious expectations of

themselves and of the parish—of their own personal needs in seeking
to join, and the true nature of the assistance the congreagation has to
offer.

One final way of looking at the process of organizational socialization
is to recognize that "in approaching any new organization, an individual
makes two classes of decisions—a decision to join and a decision to
participate."[14] The initial psychological contract may affirm that the
individual will see himelf as a member, but this is not the same thing
as a contract to participate. I recall vividly during my time in the military
some men who had made this type of contract. They had little control
over the decision to join the military service, but they could still control
the degree to which they would participate. The same two choices are
before every new organization member. This can be a very helpful
distinction. One congregation in a basically mobile community noticed
that the people in it who were participating in one or more congregational activity were 80 percent people with at least five years' membership. This led them to see that the church had only one activity which
was really open to newcomers. All its other organizations were so tightly
knit as to make entry extremely difficult. The church had a very open
door on the level of a decision to join; it had many closed doors on the
level of a decision to participate. By failing in the past to examine all
aspects of the process by which a person attached himself to the congregation they had previously failed to uncover a major reason for a falloff
in commitment, involvement, and motivation.

KEEPING THE PSYCHOLOGICAL CONTRACT VALID

The psychological contract between an individual and the organization cannot be drawn up once and then placed in a safety-deposit box
for safekeeping. The contract is dynamic, and opportunities must be
present for continual communication and renegotiation. How to do this
well, with rapidity and clarity, given the diversity and immense range
of our society, is a problem. The invention and use of adequate processes
to accomplish this are imperatively needed by our major institutions.

The complexity of the social problems that confront us, the loss of traditional sources of authority, and the absence of unifying symbols and myths make it an urgent task.

A particularly compelling example is the process of liturgical reform and Prayer Book revision which has been a central concern for the Episcopal Church in recent years. The impetus for these changes has come from a world-wide liturgical movement in Roman Catholic and Protestant bodies. This has had many diverse and important sources, such as a renewed interest in biblical theology and the strength of ecumenical conversation. Nevertheless, the major imperative for liturgical reform has been and still is, the sense that the church is in a battle to retain its capacity to communicate with Western man. A widely utilized study guide to proposed Prayer Book revision states the cause this way: "The deepest reason that the forms of worship in the church are changing is that the assumptions that go together to make up our world have radically changed since the time the first Book of Common Prayer was written."[15] That first Prayer Book went into use in 1549. Things have changed since, but I grew up in an Episcopal Church where "the Prayer Book" (in this case a 1928 version) was the symbol of our identity. I was told, I believed, and I experienced the fact that Anglican diversity was possible because of the unity of our Prayer Book. The words of its ritual became over the years as much a part of me as my own name. To alter it is to make a major change and intervention in the life and fabric of the Episcopal Church.

In 1971 and 1972 the process of change was in full swing. Several hundred thousand copies of the "Green Book," as the volume of *Services for Trial Use* became known, were in use throughout the Episcopal Church.[16] Quite naturally the widespread trial use of these new forms of worship has caused great turmoil. "Words cannot adequately describe the depth of the grief I feel at the substitution of the new, fat, Green Book liturgies for the old that I knew and loved so well."[17] "In Florida we have a great many winter visitors from all over the country. In this parish we use the Prayer Book. During the past season very visitor without exception who commented on the service rejoiced to find the

Prayer Book Mass here. Also without exception they deplored the trial liturgies."[18]

Moving from parish to parish I began to notice that some congregations were filled with apathy or outright dissent over trial use. Anger at the national church, the diocese, or the rector for creating this mess was deep and widespread. Still other parishes, however, seemed to be working through a period of trial use with comparatively little discord and sometimes with real excitement. Why the difference? Why were some congregations maintaining the psychological contract with regard to worship while others were rife with distrust and disharmony. I found I could not easily account for the difference. It was certainly not that one parish was conservative and another liberal, or one "high church" and another "low church," or simply that one had a better promotional or educational program than another. As in all questions of member participation and leadership influence, I began to realize that here the issues were systemic and would be complex and difficult to isolate.

The first clue came from a suburban, family-oriented congregation in the South. Its leadership first became sensitive to a need to be aware of the congregation's expectations because of doubt and confusion concerning the future form of the church's Christian education program. In the process of consulting with the congregation on this problem, I assisted them in designing a Sunday morning session to take a partial reading on the psychologial contract of a large segment of the congregation. Some 130 adults in small discussion groups answered the question: In your role as parent and/or member of St. Luke's what would make your life in this church more rewarding for you? The question is designed to give persons an opportunity to talk about what they expect but do not receive—both intrinsically and extrinsically—from participation in the life of the church. It very carefully does *not* ask what people think the church ought to be or do. The directions to the small group emphasize the importance of allowing each individual to have his say. Consensus is not wanted. Relevance comes from the patterning and frequency of personal, individual responses rather then homogenized group reports.

The answers revealed a surprising and large area of concern with the worship of the church.

"I will be relieved when our church decides what kind of service we will use."
"Hymns are difficult to sing."
"Too much confusion in the services. Let us get a new service—fix it and get on with it."
"Be better if less group discussions—some things should be passed down as instruction. Let vestry or those in charge—go ahead and take action with results dictating change."
"Service more unstructured—throw away the books."
"Maybe change is not good—maybe we come here to stay away from change."
"I don't like the disorder of the new service—very displeased."
"Like the order of service now, but could leave sermon out of 8:30 group."
"It does not matter really how we feel—they are going to do what they want to anyway."

These seemingly contradictory, emotionally laden comments were enough to force me to think about the basic ingredients of an individual's psychological contract with the church in the area of worship. Erik Erikson, as much as any modern thinker, has tried to establish the connections between man's institutions and the early, individual developmental experience of a person. In an article on the development of ritualization Erikson traces out why he believes ritual is an emotional and practical necessity for human development.[19] He suggests that the ontogenetic source of ritual is in the ceremonial of the nursery. The process is familiar to every parent. The hallowed ritual of early morning greeting between infant and mother—the glow of mutual recognition and care—the unvarying stereotyped exchange of words and actions. For mother and child a moment of emotional and practical necessity fusing love and physical care into a ceremony that affirms the child's uniqueness and overcomes his apartness.

I began to think about the bedtime ritual with my own sons. My five-year-old has a ritual that is unfailing in its constancy. I would not dream of sitting in a different chair to read his bedtime story or of leaving out any elements of the ceremony—nor would my son easily allow such variation. I also began to recognize the mutuality of our needs. At a time in evening when I often wished to settle down—to be done with the demands of the day—the bedtime ritual provided for me a formalized structure in which I could overcome my own ambivalence and express care and love.

Suddenly I realized that one thing the people of St. Luke's were saying is that the element of familiarity through repetition—the creativity that derives from the stylized, repetitive formality of ritual—was being destroyed. Never knowing what to expect, the encountering of constant and surprising change, were in fact eroding the deepest psychic bases of what people sought in worship.

I took another look at the congregations that had the least difficulty with the trauma of liturgical change and discovered that they were congregations which had taken care not to violate the ritual nature of worship. Most parishes had made efforts to educate their congregation about the reasons for Prayer Book revision and the outlines of the process of trial use and evaluation. These efforts to inform do not necessarily say anything to a person's sense of certainty or uncertainty. Unflagging effort to provide a sense of sureness—to do all things possible to alleviate a sense of "What next?"—I could now see as essential. One successful congregation used continual, redundant means of communication to tell people what service to expect, how to find their way through it, and how long they could expect to experience any one change.

The functional reason for being careful to maintain the formalized familiarity—the expected standard patterns of ritual—is that it provides a structure for the overcoming of uncertainty, of ambivalent attitudes or feelings. The bedtime ritual with my son provides a way for both of us to get through a time of the evening filled with powerful competing emotions. He needs to go to bed and rest; he wants help, but wants to exert his independence. I want to know him, him to know me, yet I want some time for myself. I want him to take care of himself, but don't want to stand around all night while he dawdles and plays; he wants love and care and is angry at the powerful man who takes over at this moment the love and affection of the woman in the house. These issues are real for me and my son each night. The bedtime ritual enables us to live through them. I would hate to have to discuss, debate, and explore these dynamics every evening. I believe this is part of what people mean when they say, "We are coming here to get away from change."

"All week I deal with frustration and conflict. Why do I have to on Sunday in the worship of Almighty God?" When the clergy belabor the laity for such feelings I believe they are denying the fact that part of the Good News of worship is the overcoming confusion and uncertainty. There was an article in a recent edition of a church newspaper which discussed the packed-pew success of a conservative congregation. It quoted a member as saying, "There is a refreshing consistency here every week. The services have dignity appropriate to a house of God—and you aren't always wondering what's going to happen next by way of Micky Mouse liturgical stunts."[20]

Consistency and dignity are functionally essential. The person who said at St. Luke's, "Let's get a new service—fix it and get on with it," is saying you are cheating on the contract—you are robbing me of some of the elements of worship which are essential for me.

An emphasis on the changing, variable, and intangible nature of the psychological contract and the institutional dilemma of maintaining a trustworthy contract with a wide range of persons leads to the consideration of additional factors. The authority of the institution—the army, the university, the church—can no longer assure compliance, much less commitment. Commitment involves cooperative endeavor based on congruence between individual interest and organizational goals. The loss of power to insure compliance results in organizations having to deal with conflicts of interest—varieties of psychological contracts—in the hope of securing commitment. It is a situation which suggests "different strokes for different folks" as an organizational stance. It also suggests that leadership must understand the psychology of power and politics in situations pregnant with conflicting interest. My younger son's bedtime ritual was wildly disrupted some evenings back when he felt himself in competition, in a conflict of interest with his older brother. He was comparing his power in the family with his brother's, and he took the fight into his bedtime routine. I do not think the connection between power conflict and bedtime ritual was accidental. And I think it is no accident that the worship of the church has become a focal point of conflicts of interest and struggles for power. In a common-sense fashion I think most of us are aware that to tamper with a person's ritual is akin to treading on sacred ground. I don't expect my son to calmly and rationally discuss changes in our more sacred family routines. Look back at the comments of the people at St. Luke's and notice the recurring references to who has the authority and power to decide. "It does not really matter how you feel—they are going to do what they want anyway."

The church should not expect participative planning procedures to carry the burden of change. No matter how participative the procedures, mistrust of the intent of the leadership is likely to be present, particularly in areas fraught with symbolic content. The personal issues are far too deep to be managed easily through opinion polls or mutual goal-setting processes.

These deep issues of power and psychic investment and their relation to the puzzle of liturgical change became evident in a visit to another parish which was coping well with trial use of the Episcopal Green Book. This is the congregation headed by the Rev. James Green, the rector whose motto is "different strokes for different folks." On a typical Sunday morning the individual parishioner is able to make his own choice with regard to the form of service. Generally two simultaneous services are held—one contemporary in form and substance, the other traditional. The two congregations come together for the sermon. The coffee hour following the services is a formalized affair in which one may expect a discussion at round tables seating ten or twelve persons, with coffee at the table. A ritual which, by the way, frees me from the fixed-smile anxieties of a stand-up, mill-around-cocktail-party, quick-find-a-familiar-face type of coffee hour. The discussion on this particular Sunday was focused on the new wording used in the Green Book as contrasted with the 1928 Prayer Book. After the table discussions there was a general discussion period with questions addressed to the rector. Several remarks were highly critical of the changes in wording which had been made in the service. This flow of comment was interrupted by a woman who asked, "Why do we always have the contemporary service here in the parish hall and not the church itself?" The rector paused a moment and answered clearly and firmly, "In my over-all reading of the mixture of people and interests this seems to make the best sense—I am somewhat conservative about the pace of change and in the final analysis I have to make the decision. I am glad to know your response and can understand your feelings, but I think it is important for now that we continue in a consistent fashion."

From this distance and on paper the woman's question seems mild, but at the time it changed the atmosphere of the room. It raised a conflict of interest and instantly triggered emotional response. It seemed to say, If those conservatives are going to have their say about the wording changes, I want my say about the second-rate allocation of space to the liberals who want a "swinging" service. The rector's reply was brilliant. In an instant I knew that he knew he was in charge, that he would not use his power capriciously, that we would not be thrown into a debilitating debate over whose interest came first, that he was not going to enter into collusion with one group against another, that he saw his power as coming from a coalition that drew upon the aggregation of our diverse interests. He seemed to have no need to side with one group or another, or to impose some penultimate solution upon us all. All this was happening within a structure which allowed me to have a voice and to explore my own understandings. The structure and the rector's leadership suggested that there is no magical, religiously ideal best way. The setting respected my need for structure and my need to explore. If I use my bedtime ritual with my son always to avoid the issues between us—so as never to explore the ambivalence of love and antagonism between father and son—then the ritual is misused. The congregation was honoring my needs for both order and exploration. The rector maintained the psychological contract and took effective leadership because he understood clearly the nature of the life drama in which he was engaged. The transactions between minister and people, between leader and member, particularly in an area of high symbolic content such as ritual and worship are likely to be laden with deep psychic expectations only dimly recognizable by the participants.

Dr. Abraham Zaleznik has stated that embedded in the operations of power and authority in an organization are three themes which shape the way power is used and distributed. Speaking as a psychiatrist, he points to the patterns of unconscious forces which swirl like an unseen magnetic storm through the processes of organizational life. Part of the uniqueness and excitement of the church derives from the fact that these "life dramas" are far more likely to surface and be visibly present here than in most other organizational situations. He suggests that a key to the improvement of organizational life lies in a correct understanding of these three themes by the leadership.

"The *first* portrays stripping the powers of a *parental figure.*" The point here is that authority figures are often responded to, not for who they are or what they are doing but rather as authorities per se. There is a common human tendency to put the authority, the symbolic parent figure, on the spot.

"The *second* portrays the predominance of *paranoid thinking,* where distortions of reality result from the surfacing of conflict which formerly had been contained in collusion." Here Dr. Zaleznik is suggesting the need for a constant awareness of the human tendency to be suspicious and often hostile toward the outsider—the other fellow. Programs emanating from national offices intended for the local scene must bear the weight of suspicion that "they" have hidden motives and that "they" do not understand our situation.

"The *third* portrays a *ritualistic ceremonial* in which real power issues are submerged or isolated in compulsive behavior but at the cost of real problem solving and work."[21] In this third theme Dr. Zaleznik points to the inclination of people to resort to ritualized procedures—"the regulations say so, that's why"—rather than bring to the surface the emotions and anxiety connected with a look at the issues involved between leader and member; supervisor and worker; parent and child.

The incident I have described contained all three dramas. The rector's response served to reassure me as to his wise use of power as the central authority figure. Worries about the other guy—what "they" want—were dispelled. A problem-solving approach was indicated rather than an easy appeal to symbolic authority whether theological or organizational (i.e., "a student of the early church would know" or "the Bishop has said"). My belief is that the symbolic structuring of the orders of the church emphasizes the authority—object role of the clergy. The life dramas which Dr. Zaleznik describes are present in every organization, but perhaps nowhere in greater strength than in the church, and nowhere within the church more centrally than in the contextual concerns of worship. Awareness and understanding of these issues renders more possible a setting in which valid, undistorted information can be exchanged between leader and member.

Leader effectiveness and member motivation are a covenant. They are joined in an indissoluble bond. It is a relationship of trust and personal influence. It is a relationship where power and authority count. It is an agreement affected by the *job to be done*. The conditions for leader effectiveness and member commitment are multiple, interlocking, and systemic in nature. In particular the attention paid to the psychological contract; to the diversity of orientations and needs which people bring to the organization; to the continuous sensing of these differences; to creation of exciting tasks responsive to those needs; and to a knowing, judicious use of power and influence—these constitute useful avenues for increased vitality.

1. Abraham Maslow, *Motivation and Personality* (New York: Harper & Row, 1954), pp. 80–106.

2. Quoted in the *Washington Post*, November 24, 1972, p. 1 from a research report at the University of Michigan.

3. Frederick Herzberg, *Work and the Nature of Man* (Cleveland: World Publishing Co., 1966), pp. .

4. Robert N. Ford, *Motivation Through the Work Itself* AMA, 1969, p. 91.

5. Dave H. Fenn, Jr., "Executives as Community Volunteers," *Harvard Business Review*, (March-April 1971), p. 4.

6. Paul R. Lawrence, "How to Deal with Resistance to Change," *Harvard Business Review* (January-February 1969), p. 4.

7. Thomas E. Bier, "Contemporary Youth: Implications of the Personalistic Life Style for Organizations," Ph.D. diss. (Case Western Reserve University, 1967), p. .

8. Fenn, op. cit., p. 156.

9. Ibid., p. 16.

10. Interview with James R. Green, Rector, Resurrection Church, Alexandria, Va.

11. Irwin Rubin, David Kolb, James McIntyre, and George Farris, "The Process of Joining Up Individuals and Organizations," *Educational Opportunity Forum* 2, no. 1 (Albany, N.Y.: University of the State of New York, Division of Higher Education, 1969).

12. See Edgar H. Schien, "Organizational Socialization and the Profession of Management," *Industrial Management Review* (Winter 1968).

13. Ibid., p. 4.

14. Rubin, *et al.*, op. cit., p. 2.

15. Alfred R. Shands and H. Barry Evans, *How and Why* (New York: Seabury Press, 1971), p. 15.

16. *Services for Trial Use* (New York: The Church Hymnal Corporation, 1971).

17. Watson Parker, "a Parishioner to His Rector," *The Living Church,* July 16, 1972, p. 10.

18. Letter to the editor from J. E. Massie, Arcadia, Florida, printed in *The Living Church,* July 30, 1972, p. 3.

19. Erik Erikson, "The Development of Ritualization," in *The Religious Situation,* Donald R. Cutler (Boston: Beacon Press, 1968).

20. *American Church News* (Summer 1972), p. 10, quoting an article by Lester Kinsolving, Religion Editor, *San Francisco Chronicle.*

21. Abraham Zaleznik, "Power and Politics in Organizational Life," *Harvard Business Review* (May-June 1970), p. 53.

5

Roles and Role Relationships

When clergy gather, one of the "in house" sayings is, "When is a businessman not a businessman?" Answer: "When he is on a church board." The riddle expresses the frustration many clergy feel when they see experienced, successful, talented businessmen spending valuable hours debating issues of trivial consequence for the life of the church. What is surprising is that this same complaint is expressed by the professional leadership in other volunteer organizations. Research by the Center for a Voluntary Society has revealed that it is widely true that when a businessman enters any volunteer agency he "leaves his leadership hat outside the door—even in areas he knows best and likes best."[1] The directors of these volunteer agencies sound just like the local clergy in lamenting the failure of the business executive to grapple with basic

74

procedures and policies, expending their valuable energies instead on day-to-day routine matters. The research establishes a real breakdown in communication between volunteer and paid professional. While the majority of business leaders feel underutilized and that their real skills and abilities are not being tapped, the paid staff grieve over the lack of leadership and creativity provided by the volunteers. Neither seems to know what the other wants and expects.

THE CONCEPT OF ROLE RELATIONSHIPS

The concept, derived from the theater, of role and role exceptations, is a powerful tool for understanding the way social systems cohere and function. The theater is one of the most effective means man has created of capturing the drama of life, of portraying the mystery, excitement, and intensity of human relationships. It helps us to see the patterns and forces of life on the stage before us in a way which eludes us in day-to-day experience. In a similar fashion role theory enables us to move beyond static descriptions of organizational realities to begin to sense and describe the patterned forces and processes which link the members of an organization in the dramas of their work. When a person reads for a part in a play he is handed a script which contains dialogue and stage directions. These are the author's expectations for the role. Under the impact of interaction with the director and the remainder of the cast (the role set) the role is further defined. If the person does well in the role, then eventually there will be interaction with an audience and drama critics (the relevant environment), providing additional inputs by which the actor creates with his talent an exciting role for himself.

A similar process continually occurs in every social system. A function must be performed, information is exchanged about expectations; if the person takes on the role, then a period of productive activity is entered into on the basis of perceived expectations, and then, as additional information enters the picture, expectations for the role shift, and those involved are forced to some type of accommodation. This process of establishing roles is in many ways the basic glue of social systems. The recurrent patterned activities of a role position together with the corresponding role pressures and expectations account for much of the stability that characterizes organizational life.

Organizations are quite complex—there is no one author of the play and the dialogue; the work a person is expected to perform can never be spelled out in a written script. Individuals in a social system must cope with the fact that they have multiple roles. For each role there is a different cast of characters with whom they must relate. All the relevant persons immediately influencing even one role (the role set) are not easily assembled on a stage seeking clarification from a director. "Messages" from the environment are seldom as unambiguous or as timely and direct as an audience's applause or a drama critic's review in the early edition. This complexity is far more critical than the physical size of an organization. The more complex, varied, and numerous the role relationships, the larger the organization in the most profound sense of bigness.

When a businessman takes the role of volunteer in a community agency, he is adding to the multiple role obligations which constantly impinge on his life. He is putting himself in the position of having to sort out that role, resolve probable conflicts with his other roles, choose between possible conflicting role pressures from the role set, and add to the continued role transititions he must make. The businessman may find that his own values conflict with what he perceives to be the obligations of his new role. He is, in short, freshly encountering the enormous complexity of role systems in organizations.

ROLE AMBIGUITY AND ORGANIZATIONAL DIFFUSION

As the example of volunteer agencies illustrates, a high degree of ambiguity is not unusual in any social system with regard to role expectations. One thing the church shares with other volunteer organizations is a widespread organizational diffusion in both space and time. People in an office or plant interact eight hours a day, five days a week. There is a confined intensity of interaction about the usual business organization which provides continuing opportunity for communication and clarification of expectations to occur. In the church and in most volunteer agencies the interaction is much more diffuse. The volunteer board member may spend only two hours a month in the role. His contact with others within the volunteer work setting from whom he might get cues about his role is usually sparse and intermittent. He may never get a chance physically to see the organization in operation at one time in one place. Cues similar to those that come from the physical layout and from visual observation of the flow of work in an office or plant are seldom available as information sources to the volunteer. Much of the work of a church does not transpire within the confines of the physical plant but in homes, hospitals, on the street, or in a restaurant. Behind the old joke "What do you clergy do the other six days of the week?" lies the reality that it is difficult for the average church member to form an adequate visual or mental picture of a clergyman's work. It is a piece of the mystery entitled, What goes on around here, and what part am I expected to play?

Much of the stability and productivity of a social system depends on clear, unambiguous patterning of role and role expectations. This clarity is necessary for freely chosen commitment to a role and for creative expression within that role. The widespread failure of businessmen to be businessmen in a volunteer position is a symptom of the need for the church and other volunteer organizations to pay serious attention to the processes by which role expectations are communicated and clarified.

CHANGING THE SYSTEM RATHER THAN THE PERSON

Other symptoms of the same problem are close at hand. A mountain of data is now available detailing the confusion and discord present between clergy and laity over the role of the clergyman.[2] There is an important clue in this problem which I believe is vital. Christian theology and seminary training stress and teach an ideal role model. An emphasis is placed upon descriptions of how a clergyman *ought* to be in his role. The graduation address given recently at a leading seminary is a typical example. The bishop who spoke gave an eloquent word picture of the kind of role he felt these men should fulfill. It was a powerful sermon—and I am certain that it again reinforced in the minds of these new clergy a tendency to view role confusion and conflict as due to their own personal betrayal of the ideal role. It is a tremendous disservice to young clergy to be continually provided with the "oughts" of the clergyman as preacher, pastor, and prophet. The result is that those who get into role difficulties invariably blame themselves.[3] They see the problem as always being something wrong with them rather than considering the possibility that what is wrong is a systemic or organizational failure. After you have plugged ten different electrical applicances into the same wall socket and each one successively blows a fuse, it is time to assume that there is something amiss with the electrical wiring system rather than with all ten appliances. The communication processes of the church cannot handle the load. Clergy of all kinds and sizes are blowing fuses, and it is time to notice the deficiencies in the social system rather than focusing exclusively on the inability of clergy to realize an ideal role model.

The complexity and intensity of role phenomena in our institutions calls out for a process of change which is itself focused upon the processes by which organizations standardize role behavior. Unless the patterns of the organization's role relationships are changed, the influence of training or other efforts at change directed at the individual will be substantially negated by the abiding forces of his organizational roles. These forces are enormous. It is true that we tend to become the role we enact. This facet of the situation is the clearest instance I know of the potential gain from a systemic rather than individual change strategy. It is time to pay normative attention to the crucial events and processes through which role expectations are transmitted and clarified.

John Sherwood and John Glidewell have provided a simple, clear, four-step model describing the basic aspects of the way in which role relations are established. These four steps are:

1. Sharing information and negotiating expectations.
2. Commitment (deciding to take on the role).
3. Stability and productivity (a period of stable work together).
4. Disruption (due to the inevitable violation of expectations either because information is never fully transmitted or the situation changes).[4]

These four steps occur in the establishment of any set of role relationships. They describe processes continually occurring in every social system. Most of the time the process is assumed and little conscious, planned effort is given to any phase. Marriage is a good example. Among the many consciousness-raising aspects of the Women's Lib movement has been a real emphasis placed on the need for husband and wife to work out a clear marriage contract. Women's Lib has quite correctly noticed that unless husband and wife self-consciously exchange information and share expectations, each will become the captive of cultural expectations about their respective roles. Unspoken cultural assumptions haunt the relationship and lead to unproductive disruptions. By contracting with one another, committing themselves to the contracts and expecting to use periods of disruption in the normal course of the marriage as times for further clarification, husband and wife avoid some of the confusion based on stereotyped assumptions and are better able to identify actual role conflicts.

Notice two crucial points about this example, for they apply to every social system. They are as applicable to a lay volunteer on a church committee as to a marriage. First, every man and woman going into a marriage has a set of assumptions about his or her new role. (This is also true of each person entering an organization.) A certain amount of information is always exchanged about those assumptions. A person's freedom and capacity for commitment are directly related to their clarity and congruity. Women's Lib, the changing role of men and women, new views of marriage, and the phenomenal stresses now placed

upon the nuclear family make it almost certain that husband and wife
will not share a neat, tidy cultural picture of their role relationship for
more than a short period of time—if at all. They are likely, in fact, to
have widely differing and rapidly changing views of what they expect
from one another. The members of a church board are just as likely to
differ in the expectations they initially bring to their roles on that board.

In the past it may have been possible to make reasonably valid assumptions about great segments of the marriage relationship. It is apparent that today commitment and productivity in a marriage depend upon
a conscious normative decision to exchange this kind of information.
The point is that these comments apply equally well to a great many
other institutions besides the family. The relations between college
faculty and students, between pastor and people, between board members, between army officers and troops have been in the past largely
assumed. In each case we now know that cultural osmosis is no longer
a sufficient channel for a sound working relationship. The information
people bring to the original roles is not sufficient to build a stable
working relationship.

The second critical point of the example is that disruption will always
happen. The issue is whether or not the occurrence of static in the
situation leads to a planned renegotiation or to termination of the
relationship or withdrawal from it. Marriage is a particularly useful
example, for it brings home the way in which disruption can seem like
betrayal and the enormous anxiety generated when the role relationship
feels in jeopardy. The instinctive wish is to return things to "normal"
—to get rid of bad feelings rather than using the time of crunch as an
occasion to clarify expectations and renegotiate the roles, using the
information generated in the bind.

It is possible, in a social system, to anticipate where some of the binds
will arise. It is also possible to become skillfully aware of the early
warning signals which are precursors of a storm of disruption. By responding early, much of the conflict and distress of disruption can be
avoided. Institutional leaders need to pay direct attention to the process
by which role relationships are established, make a self-conscious initial

contract, look for early signs of discord, and plan to use it as a period for renegotiation. Here is an example of that advice in operation. A congregation was using the services of two parish development consultants in association with Project Test Pattern. Working with a liaison committee, the consultants had gathered interview data concerning the climate of the congregation. On the basis of this information the committee developed an objective for two weekend conferences of the parish clergy and lay leadership which was stated as: "to come to the place where we can agree on expectations, not just intellectually, but on a feeling level, both for the clergy and staff and for the laity."

The two resulting conferences were quite successful and contained three different types of activity. First, the consultants presented a theoretical model which explained the meaning of and necessity for a clear psychological contract with the total membership, a sound professional contract with the staff, and a firm administrative contract for each project undertaken by the leadership. Clear contracting on all three levels was suggested as a procedure for achieving clarity of expectations.

The second activity of these workshops consisted of the leadership's bringing to the surface their expectations about their own roles and the support they desired from one another. The discussion used such questions as:

What are the characteristics of a good vestry member?
Are they operative in your fellow members?
What is your stake or investment in the work of the vestry?
What kinds of supportive behavior do you want from members of the vestry?

The third activity was to put the theory and shared expectations to work in exploring and making decisions about their implications for the way leadership actually functioned. A typical comment by the leadership about these sessions was: "For me personally this was the greatest eye-opener in my career as a leader. By frankly centering the questionnaires around the role of the rector I suddenly saw and was able to analyze and discuss the problems of leadership and contractual misunderstandings that had been observed under less direct diagnosis previously." Another individual said that the workshops had led to an "acceptance by the vestry and wardens of responsibility for important functions of parish life and for support of the rector in a real way in implementing goals." The success of the workshops was due in part, I believe, to the fact that they took place before the issues had become intolerably divisive.

Crucial moments for the establishment and solidification of effective role relationships are apparent in the systemic life of a congregation. Here are some of the most important:

- When a new pastor is chosen.
- Whenever someone is asked to serve on a committee or task force.
- When there is a reorganization.
- Whenever there is a significant change in congregational direction.
- When a new staff member is hired—the planned renegotiation should include the total staff.
- In periodic evaluation of the clergyman's work.
- When people are beginning to notice discontent with the leadership and *before* things have reached the stage of open conflict and disruption.
- When the minister wishes to significantly alter his own work priorities—as in taking on a large time commitment to a project outside the church.

Identification of these key points for negotiation does no good unless they are made use of on a normal, continuing basis as hygienic, preventive maintenance for the organization. My experience is that this is seldom done. Congregational leaders wait until there is a violent, bitter dispute before deciding it is time to seek a settlement. This is generally too late. Like a lot of other things, the disruption of role relationship is far more easily treated in the initial stages. Once the conflict has moved into an advanced stage the chances for a renegotiation of roles in which there will be widespread trust and commitment are slight. Again, just as in marriage, our organizational tendency seems to be to hope the trouble will blow over and we can return to things as they were. But faced early enough, what feels like conflict often turns out to be the result of misperception—of ambiguity due to inadequate, distorted communication of role expectations.[5] The consequences of continuing ambiguity are in the long run as disabling as actual conflict.

This is more than abstract theory. The *so what* is that these forces do operate. The calling of a new minister is a vivid example. The role expectations a congregation has of its chief pastor are shaped by their experience with the incumbent. When a man departs after ten years as the local minister he leaves behind him a strong set of emotional attachments which are symbolic object relationship supports for the congregational picture of the role. The process of calling a new minister must smoke out these expectations. It should provide opportunities for people to verbalize and talk through their wishes for the new man. The calling process needs to spell out the expectations people have of the chief pastor's role. To do this takes time and energy, for it means having to work simultaneously with letting go of the previous man; it also means problem-solving for the crucial needs of the congregation at this point in its life. One pastor, who was chosen by this type of process, ascribed much of his success at innovative Christian education in his new setting as due to the clarity he felt about the congregation's wish that he make this a priority of his ministry.[6] Two years later he felt the need to check out the initial contract—to renegotiate the relationship—and found that the wish was for still further concentration on Christian education, and so plunged in with renewed vigor and commitment.

In contrast to this success story is the statement of one seasoned Episcopal bishop who can trace 95% of the major clergy-lay conflicts in the history of his episcopate to initial haphazard, too-rapid, and ill-defined calling of each of these clergy by vestries who did not see the need for the ventilation and exploration of expectations by the congregation or even by themselves as the key leadership. Some congregations try to solve the problem, and feel they will thereby avoid surprises, by choosing the associate minister to succeed the minister. But the fact is,

they are often mightily surprised. They have known the assistant in
another role. Both his own expectations and those of the laity change
if he is elevated to the Number One spot. The past history together
really makes it more rather than less important to enter carefully into
a new set of role relationships.

These are some sound reasons why the church as an institution has
done so little with organizational role procedures. It is possible for use
of opportunities for role clarification to be both boring and threatening.
A couple who are just deciding to become engaged would, I am sure,
be far more interested in sealing the bargain with a kiss (or several) than
in a structured conversation exploring mutual expectations. Such a session raises the threat of a premature breaking off of the relationship and
can be a mechanical, dead procedure for examining an exciting, live
relationship. Many of us feel that there are aspects of human relationships which are like the delicate petals of a flower: they lose their beauty
by being touched, handled, and examined too closely. Indeed, it is hard
to capture in such a discussion as this the delicacy and spontaneity really
necessary to a sharing of role expectations. For instance, who has ever
been a part of a performance appraisal system that had any elements of
fun, interest, or excitement? Almost no one. And yet this is probably the
most commonly experienced procedure developed as a means of clarify-
ing and enforcing role expectations.

This mechanistic approach is one reason so little advantage is taken
of the critical points of choice for role clarification. The church is an
institution which addresses itself to the greatest and most mysterious
dimensions of life. I once heard a cold, fruitless, empty debate between
a minister and church board concerning the mechanical report he was
submitting to them listing the number of calls he made in the hospital,
hours spent in counseling, administration, etc. He had begun this time-
sheet procedure because he knew there was conflict with the board over
his style of ministry. But his choice of a mechanical procedure only
deepened the problem. It was demeaning to him personally, and is in
my opinion an almost blasphemous debasing of the church's ministry.
An occasion which might have become a mutual exploration of the

nature of ministry to the sick and dying became an angry, suspicion-filled argument over how long a hospital call should take. Phrases such as job description, work contract, or annual evaluation trigger the fear that the humaneness of our life together will be reduced to duplicate copies of bureaucratic, sterile procedures. The fear is well founded.

I hope the point is clear. Most personnel administration procedures are devices to adjust, regularize, and respond to the continuing process of role establishment and functioning which is a basic ingredient of social systems. Manuals of work procedures, job descriptions, personnel policies, and annual evaluations are all examples of attempts to institutionalize procedures which speak to the question of what we expect from one another in this setting. These basic procedures are neither good nor bad. They are analogous in my mind to nude portraits. Some of our greatest art and sculpture depict the nude human form. Other portrayals of the human form are simply pornography. Many of these regularized procedures become bureaucratic pornography, trampling upon the uniqueness of human relationships. At the same time, each of the procedures named arose out of a genuine human need to clarify expectations and provide information channels for continued role negotiation. This qualitative distinction marking the fragile mystery of human life must be kept in the foreground of all role clarification efforts.

1. Dave H. Fenn, Jr., "Executives as Community Volunteers," *Harvard Business Review* (March-April 1971), p. 15.

2. Jeffrey K. Hadden, *The Gathering Storm in the Churches: The Widening Gap Between Clergy and Laymen* (Garden City, N.Y.: Doubleday & Co., 1969).

3. Edgar Mills and John P. Koval, *Stress in the Ministry*, IDOC document (New York: 1971).

4. John J. Sherwood and John C. Glidewell, *Planned Renegotiation: A Norm-Setting OD Intervention*, paper no. 338 (Lafayette, Ill.: Graduate School of Industrial Administration, Purdue University, 1971).

5. See James D. Anderson, "Pastoral Support of the Clergy-Role Development within Local Congregations," in *Pastoral Psychology* (March 1971) pp. 9-14

6. See James D. Anderson, "Finding the Problem" in *Colloquy on Christian Education*, ed. John Westerhoff (Philadelphia: Pilgrim Press, 1972) pp. 213-19.

6

Conflict

In a recent program of continuing education for mid-career clergy of several denominations I presented the case study of a changing congregation. It described the reasonably successful thirty-month effort of this church to manage some significant issues of dissent, apathy, decline, and withdrawal. The part of the study which the continuing education students found most exciting was the way the local pastor had changed his leadership style in responding to conflict or resistance. They quickly identified their own leadership style with his initial way of handling conflict by passive withdrawal, avoidance, and instant efforts at reconciliation. They were excited by the positive results that transpired when the rector began to work with resistance, analyzing what was happening, seeking people out, trying to hear and be heard. Their excitement at this change was understandable. Research and experience show that they were identifying in themselves and in the study a common and crucial leadership problem present in any organization undergoing stress and change. The problem is how leaders respond to conflict and resistance within their organization.

Marvin Dunnette and John Campbell in an article published in the *Industrial Relations Journal* summarize their observations of a number of managers in distressed organizations with these comments:

> Most managers . . . tended to show apathy or belligerence. Some were consistently apathetic, others consistently belligerent, but most behaved inconsistently, ranging from apathy (withdrawal) to belligerent aggressiveness (attack) from situation to situation. They tended to spend too much time pressing for quick action in response to difficulties. More often than not, they ended up responding inappropriately and non-constructively to the problems and threats facing them.[1]

These characteristics of anxious belligerence, withdrawal, and a strong wish to remove the sources of distress and achieve tranquility are extremely familiar patterns in the church as well as other institutions. Few of us imagine that we do well in conflict and yet the times seem to call for effective use of it.

THE NATURE OF CONFLICT

Conflict is not an easy phenomenon to understand. When we speak of it in our institutions, images come to mind: a strident group of students invading the college president's office, fighting between white and black in an overcrowded army barracks, an angry dispute between minister and members over the social stance of the church. These mixed images point to the varied understandings of conflict present in our commonplace thought. The word is used to describe military combat, ideological argument, active dissent, emotional strife, controversial debate; open, active hostility; internal stress; and vindictive, lingering animosity. We use the word to describe actions, attitudes, and feelings between nations, groups, individuals, and even within an individual. I am helped by understanding that this confusion of meanings exists. It is simply true that there is no one tidy set of human phenomena we can label precisely "conflict."

My own understanding is simply that conflict is a natural and expected element in human affairs which arises because of differences.[2] If two people differ over an intellectual concept, then the conflict is expressed as a disagreement. In politics the opposition party expresses its differences in values and concept by political conflict. Basic to this conflict is the difference in power between the parties.

Differences are inevitable. They may concern power, prestige, reward, values, goals, methods, perceptions, or factual definitions. The response to those differences may be analysis, fighting, argument, debate, withdrawal, subversion, a search for compromise or attempts at repression. Conflict is the response to and expression of differences. Moreover, we each have a characteristic style of perceiving, responding to, and expressing differences. The manner in which differences were expressed and conflict emerged in our families, constitutes our earliest and most important training in conflict utilization. Conflict situations hook us on a deep emotional basis, reawakening early childhood experiences of difference between parent and child. We associate emotionally the oppositions that emerge in conflict with the primal issues between parent and child. Differences between boss and subordinate, male and female, black and white, engineer and artist are inevitable. As social systems and as individuals we have developed characteristic ways of perceiving, expressing and responding to those differences. This is our individual and systemic style of conflict management. We live in a culture in which the suppression of differences by those in power—parent, superior, teacher, social class or nation—has been a strong influence on our choice of conflict management style.

Take for example Pastor Smith, who was greatly concerned about a "conflict" he was experiencing. A small group in the congregation seemed to him to be opposed to everything he wanted. The budget, which he felt had been amply reviewed in the finance committee, was hotly contested at the following meeting of the congregational board. The pastor's every emotion was to rid himself of the conflict. He was not able, even with help, to be skillful in understanding what was happening or to stay in touch with the impact of his own behavior on the other people involved. His personally unacceptable anger at being opposed was expressed as cold withdrawal and hurt feelings. In the stress of the conflict the pastor reverted to old and unproductive ways of responding to those who differed with him. The result was that some of the "opposition" left the congregation and others simply became quiet. The minister then began to express his concern over the dull, drab, lifeless apathy of the board meetings.

In this case the pastor had used his considerable powers of approval and disapproval to suppress differences and hence rid himself of the conflict. He found that this had a cost. The example is dramatically familiar. The Rev. Hans Scherner, a Lutheran clergyman who has helped to lead a conflict utilization program for clergy for the last three years, says that in general he feels the clergy attending are seeking to remove the distress caused by conflict rather than looking for help to accomplish positive goals. Primarily they seem to "want to deal with the bad feelings and get to more peace."[3] These observations fit the findings of Campbell and Dunnette concerning managers in industry. It is important for church people to recognize that this trait is not unique to the clergy. Professor J. S. Livingston of the Harvard Business School has commented that management graduates suffer their worst trauma when they find that human emotions as well as rational thought processes are a part of solving management problems.[4]

CONFLICT AS A SYSTEMIC PROBLEM

Conflict is a major problem for social systems first, then, because the emotions it raises are a problem for most individuals. Our fight training is usually limited to our own family experience. Most of us have been overexposed to people in power who tended to suppress differences rather than deal with the threat they felt conflict posed for them. The patterns by which we express and respond to differences lie deep within us and are difficult to change.

Second, conflict is a problem for organization because there are often systemic forces at work which militate against the recognition and constructive use of differences. A conflict utilization project established by the Diocese of Southern Ohio developed as its first hypothesis: "The inability of parishes to face conflict and develop constructive ways to utilize it, is caused by the existence of a norm which rejects behavior tending to open up conflict and rewards behavior which tends to suppress it."[5] Their experience in the project supported the hypothesis. One lay person in refusing to cooperate with the project said, "I refuse to fill this out. The word conflict should not be used in a church setting."[6] My guess is that the woman was saying that no matter how you feel individually, debate, disagreement, political demonstration and the voicing of opposing views have no place in church particularly if done so as to arouse ire or emotion. Without any guessing we can be certain that she is expressing the social pressures of an organizational norm. This is a very important point. I am saying that even if one learns as an individual or in the family that conflict is an inevitable part of human existence and that it is important to learn creative ways of expressing, understanding, and utilizing differences, there still remains an organizational pressure that says *No-no-not here!* The curious situation then arises in which the existence of a norm suppressing conflict in itself generates conflict.

My own family provides a clear example. As a family we are working on trying to support the expression and understanding of our differences. Recently I found myself in an intense conflict with my middle son. He kept yelling that he had no power, and I kept yelling that power was not the issue—he had broken the rules of conduct in our house. I did not want to listen to his saying the issue was power. Only gradually did it dawn on me that I was using my power to cut off understanding, and that maybe power *was* a part of our conflict. The result of the fight was a family meeting which ended by rearranging some of the decision-making procedures in our family. In halting fashion we have learned as a family the value of this type of hassle. One result has been that a new hassle or conflict is generated by the interface between our family and the schools the boys attend. In the schools a different kind of behavior is rewarded: a norm exists which rewards the suppression of these differences and rewards unquestioning obedience. Thus a significant point of tension or difference is generated between our family as a social system and the social system of the school.

I am stressing that conflict is more than an individual problem. It is a social system problem. Many institutions reward the suppression of differences. At the same time, we live in a society in which this suppression is more and more at odds with significant subsystems. In one Episcopal diocese I know there is a congregation whose ideology strongly supports a view of the church as a setting in which differences are to be aired and explored. The parish encourages the frequent use of its pulpit for the expression of controversial issues. In this respect it is completely at odds with the ideology of other congregations in the diocese who believe just as sincerely that the pulpit is not a place to air dissent and confront issues. Thus conflict ensues between these congregations because of their different styles of living with conflict.

The worst aspect of the conflict-suppression norm is that it means the social system is functioning so as to ignore part of its reality: the existence of significant differences of many types and levels between groups and between individuals. "I won't say I disagree, because I know people want this group to run smoothly." There is a growing body of research data indicating a key factor distinguishing healthy organizations is the presence of effective mechanisms for conflict management. "In high performing organizations in all environments, it was found that conflict was managed by involved individuals who dealt openly with the conflict and worked a problem until a resolution was reached which best met total organizational goals. In the effective organizations there was more of a tendency to *confront* conflict instead of using raw power to force one party's compliance or instead of smoothing over the conflict by agreeing to disagree."[7] One parish layman expressed this by saying, "There was no way we could effectively evaluate our efforts at parish program until we learned to face the conflict which arose because of our differences in values and approach."

One Protestant denomination recently conducted a study of its representatively selected growing congregations—that is parishes which were growing statistically despite the downward denominational trend. These findings were that an open dealing with issues seemed to contribute far more to congregational vitality than did a stance of conflict submergence. This certainly confirms my own experience as well as the experience of Project Test Pattern. Conflict is neither good nor bad. Choosing conflict is *not* necessarily a positive strategy for growth or maturity. On the other hand, the *avoidance* of conflict, the *submerging* of differences, and the *repression* of dissent, seem to be clear recipes for organizational ill-health.

FACILITATING THE EXPRESSION OF DIFFERENCES

Our institutions act as if they must reluctantly learn to handle conflict because it is forced upon us by our troubled society. The institutional wish remains that in some distant utopia people and social systems will learn to be smiling, congenial, and conflict-free. Not so, unless all differences are to disappear or massive repression occur. My own vision is that we will develop ways in which the expression and appreciation of differences can be harnessed to the enhancement of our corporate life.

Some steps toward this goal are:

a. To increase individual skill at analyzing the nature of existing differences, why they exist, and the way they are being handled.

b. To change the social system norm so that value is placed upon open examination of differences and valid information flows freely concerning factors surrounding a conflict situation.

c. Developing procedures in organizational problem-solving for generating and using information about the many levels and kinds of differences the social system is experiencing.

Point *a* has to do with individual skills, *b* with the climate of the organization, and *c* with the tools or structures the organization has available in conflict situations. Here is an example of each.

INDIVIDUAL CHANGE

Human beings do not change easily. At the very least, we can be certain that the motivational sources of human behavior are complex and deep. Acceptance of psychoanalytic theory suggests that the taproot of a person's identity is shaped in the first years of his life. An attempt to change the nature of the compound of behavior, attitudes, and values of any person in relation to conflict should have modest goals. Accordingly, the individual goals I am suggesting are to increase one's skill in understanding sources of conflict and to make one aware of one's own characteristic personal style of responding to it.

The Metropolitan Ecumenical Training Center in Washington has used with real success a survey of conflict management styles in its clergy training program. The survey, designed by Dr. Jay Hall, is well attuned to both goals: that of increasing diagnostic skill and that of enhancing awareness of one's reactions and responses to conflict situations.[8] The person taking the survey answers a number of questions ranking his characteristic response to a variety of the dynamics present in conflict. Use of this survey form has allowed the clergy in the METC program to build a graphic picture of their own style and to compare it with other clergy in training. The personally intriguing nature of the survey, coupled with the group interaction it facilitates, engages the learner in a practical experience of analysis and diagnosis of a variety of ways of analyzing expressions and responses to differences.

In a recent conflict with a friend and colleague I was helped to see that a part of my conflict style is to come on very powerfully—on both emotional and intellectual levels—with anger and more definiteness than I really feel. I do not expect easily to change my style, but it does help to know the impact my behavior can have on others. My experience is that by approaching a conflict situation with greater awareness of my own impact, I will be better able to understand what is happening and hence freer to respond to all aspects of the situation. This awareness of one's own characteristic responses to conflict, coupled with a conceptual framework for approaching the dynamics of conflict, is what the Jay Hall survey instrument provides.

NORM CHANGE

Without a shadow of doubt the clergyman is the influence leader in a congregation. He is the Number One opinion leader, and his approaches to conflict have dramatic effect on the parish. Obviously the clergyman is not the sole opinion leader in a congregation. The Diocese of Southern Ohio's Conflict Utilization project was able to identify ten to twenty lay opinion leaders in each test congregation. These individuals turned out to be bridge people—link persons between extremes of opinion within the congregation. They were the individuals whose opinions and views were solicited in times of crisis and stress in congregational life. Two days of training in conflict utilization was provided for these leaders and the clergy. The results were positive, but a limitation was discovered which is supported by other research. Several studies have indicated that a person receiving individual training is more able to apply the newly learned skills when there is back home support for the skills. If the culture of the organization is not supportive of the skills learned during the training they are rapidly forgotten or repressed.[9] The culture is a reflection of the assumptions people have learned and that they share concerning the behaviors valued or rewarded by the social system. Attempting to assist congregations to effectively respond to conflict by relying solely on the individual training of clergy and lay leaders will not work. The Southern Ohio Project found that they had not built in enough back-home support for the changes begun with the teams of clergy and lay opinion leaders. They found that efforts had to be made to nourish these changes by intervening in the day to day culture of the parish. As these facts indicate, training is usually better utilized when it is a means of undergirding efforts already begun to change organizational practices rather than being the means of initiating these changes. Congregations hoping to cope more effectively with conflict must learn to assess and modify the multiple ways by which the parish punishes and rewards, finds acceptable and unacceptable, the expression of differences. These congregational norms related to the expression of differences are a vital piece of parish conflict management.

One of the best examples of a norm change in the culture of an organization is the statement of a friend of mine about his family. I was talking with him about the change that had taken place in him and in his family due to their family involvement in psychotherapy. One of the man's comments was: "We fight more often but less viciously." By removing the conflict suppression norm this family no longer buries its resentments and differences until they explode with volcanic force. By repeated experiences of the value of trying to express and understand differences, they developed a new family norm supporting a more creative utilization of conflict.

The same thing can happen to organizations of other kinds. One clergyman in describing his experience with parish development consultation in Project Test Pattern reported that people were learning to question unspoken assumptions made about the culture of the organization.[10] Some valued experiences of facing differences on a deep level were making a change in the over-all climate of the parish toward conflict. He had noticed the way the atmosphere of conflict suppression supported an either-or norm in the congregation—a norm which did not leave room for the actual vast differences present among them as to the forms they wanted to see used in the church. If the suppression of conflict is valued then differences are troubling; thus the congregation was continually trying with impatient frustration to get rid of its differences by arguing: either we are an innovative parish or we are a traditional parish. As the suppression of conflict became less valuable and differences more easily aired, the leadership began to see the futility of their either-or debates and the possibilities of working creatively with their differences. They began to see the differences, the resistances, as opportunities for ministry.[11]

These norm changes in the climate or culture of this congregation were made possible by the presence in it of a team of consultants— neutral third parties who were able to provide some on-the-spot experiences of the value of airing and working with differences. Several other parishes have found that team building efforts with church boards and key committees have changed the tone of the congregation toward conflict. The board discovers at these two day conferences that their capacity to work well together is related to their capacity to express with candor their individual differences. It is this element of a strategy for change that the Southern Ohio project found it had to add in order to create fertile organizational soil for the seeds of the individual training to flourish.

STRUCTURAL CHANGE

People move and climates change, they are not stable. Structural change represents a third and essential ingredient in an effective approach to better congregational use of differences. One year's progress in upgrading individual skills and changing the congregational feel toward conflict does not mean those same changes will be around the next year. For the alteration to be stable, long-lasting, and genuinely effective there must be actual structural or procedural change in the ways and means by which the organization functions.

In the congregation I have just described, such a change might be as simple as a decision and commitment of funds to a biannual leaders' conference providing skill training in making use of the differences present in the congregation. Or procedural changes might be made in the way people are nominated and elected to church office so as to allow for greater diversity of representation and greater ease of election. The processes for incorporating new members described in Chapter 4 on membership are examples of effective procedural or structural changes affecting the congregation's capacity to utilize differences. These groups have evolved regular procedures to reward and make use of the differences which new members bring to the congregation. In a similar fashion I was suggesting in Chapter 5 that organizations can institutionalize procedures which convert the conflicts which inevitably arise in role relations into opportunities to enrich these relationships by renegotiating mutual expectations through expression of the differences which have arisen. Viewing the congregation as a social system—a dynamic, interdependent, interconnected whole—helps us to see that changes in individual skills, climate, and procedures are connecting links affecting one another. It has been proved many times that changes in work procedures, physical arrangements and job content and interaction patterns have a significant effect on the behavior and attitudes of workers.

"White sales workers who were integrated with new black workers under conditions of equal work status expressed more positive attitudes toward work place integration than non-integrated white sales clerks. Actual experience superseded learned prejudice."[12] Stable, effective, change in a congregation's over-all ability to understand and respond to differences depends not just on individual attitudes and skills or the climate of the parish; long-lasting change also involves shifts in the structures, patterns and procedures of church life. Structural change can lead to important individual changes.

One congregation I know decided that the unstable nature of the times meant that questions would inevitably arise which would generate turmoil and dissent within it. They recognized that the next issue of the metropolitan daily paper might contain a lead article about clergy arrested at the Pentagon or a National Council of Churches proclamation on abortion. Accordingly, they designed a conflict management procedure to be followed when and if such questions arose. The procedure allowed for thorough participative investigation of the facts, free access to all information brought to light; and that the various subgroups in the congregation would be heard from and the right to have minority reports was preserved. The minister's freedom to preach was safeguarded, but he also agreed to time his sermons so that his pulpit view would not come at a premature moment in the process.

The structure has functioned admirably. It provides a clear path for the expression of difference and underlines the importance to each

Christian of finding a defined, thoughtful position on the divisive public issues of the day.

Institutions in the face of conflict too often experience a failure of nerve and respond with either compulsive confrontation or frantic accommodation. Much of the research done on the church as an institution indicates that church membership in many forms tends to foster if not directly support a somewhat prejudiced, ethnocentric view of life.[13] The church is not responsible for the whole of society nor can it transform the whole of society, but we are a part of that society. We can be a faithful witness in it. By our stance in the midst of conflict— by the manner in which we understand and respond to differences of all kinds—we can witness to the eternal dignity of every human being. An institutional inability to make responsible use of conflict is in reality a coercive institutional power to obliterate the differences that constitute our uniqueness as human beings.

1. John Campbell and Marvin Dunnette, "Laboratory Education and Its Impact on Individuals," *Industrial Relations Journal* (October 1968), p. 4.

2. In particular see Warren H. Schmidt and Robert Tannenbaum, "Management and Differences," reprint no. 96 (Los Angeles: Institute of Industrial Relations, University of California, 1960).

3. Interview with the Rev. Hans Scherner, Director, Race Institute, Metropolitan Ecumenical Training Center, Washington, D.C.

4. J. S. Livingston, "The Myth of the Well Educated Manager," *Harvard Business Review* (January-February 1971), pp. 79–89.

5. George L. Reynolds for the Diocese of Southern Ohio, "Some Hypotheses Concerning Conflict in Parishes," November 12, 1971. Mimeographed.

6. Ibid., p. 1.

7. *Organizational Structure and Design*, ed. Gene W. Dalton, Paul R. Lawrence, and Jay W. Larson (Homewood, Ill.: Irwin-Dorsey Press, 1970), p. 11.

8. Jay Hall, *Conflict Management Survey* (1969). Copyright and available commercially from Teleometrics, Inc., 2200 South Post Oak Road, Houston, Texas, 77027.

9. Edwin A Fleishman, Edwin F. Harris, and Harold E. Burlt, *Leadership and Supervision in Industry: An Evaluation of a Supervisory Training Program*, monograph no. 33 (Columbus, Ohio: Bureau of Educational Research).

10. John R. Gilchrist, *An Evaluation of One Congregation's Experience with Parish Development Consultants*, Project Test Pattern occasional paper (Washington, D.C.: 1971). *Project Test Pattern* is an experimental program in parish renewal sponsored by the National Advisory Committee on Evangelism, established by the 1969 General Convention of the Episcopal Church and appointed by the Rt. Rev. John E. Hines, Presiding Bishop. The Rt. Rev. Lloyd E. Gressle, Diocese of Bethlehem is chairman of the committee. The Rev. Loren Mead is director of PTP with offices at Mount St. Alban, Washington, D. C. 20016.

11. For a useful exploration of this concept see James E. Dittes, *The Church in the Way* (New York: Charles Scribner's Sons, 1967).

12. From a study by J. Harding and R. Hogrefe, "Attitudes of White Departmental Employees toward Negro Co-workers," *Journal of Social Issues* 8, no. 1 (1952): 18–28, as quoted in *Management Training—Where Has It Gone Wrong*, ILR reprint no. 315 (Ithaca, N.Y.: New York State School of Industrial and Labor Relations, Cornell University, 1971), p. 4.

13. See James E. Dittes, "Religion, Prejudice and Personality," ch. 9 of *Research on Religious Development*, ed. Merton Strommen (Hawthorne, N.Y.: Hawthorn Books, 1971).

7

A Climate for Health

THE POWER OF THE PARISH

I had not been eager to go to the meeting. The week had been busy and I expected that the gathering of the parish planning committee would be routine. It was a familiar group, with whom I had been working for some months, and I wasn't looking for surprises. Our work however became lively. We found ourselves taking a reading on what changes had occured in the congregation during the past months. In the middle of the process one man in the group spoke up and said, "I just want you to know what has happened to me working on this committee. I have learned that it is OK to say what I am thinking and feeling. I have learned that people will accept what I have to say in this group and that it really helps our work if I don't sit on what is inside me. I've even begun doing this at work and at home and I like what has happened and the way I feel."

Driving home that night I thought about this man and the group. I remembered the first agonizing meetings of the committee, and when it seemed as if no one would speak except in the most carefully weighed and measured words. The group had felt at first that we had always to be serious, never negative, always accepting, never lightheartedly creative. Its members had seemed dull and apathetic. We had learned to have fun, to share and to understand both negative and positive feelings, to risk expressing our own thoughts and values. This man's statement reminded me of how far we had moved. It gave me a dramatic, exciting example of the power of this committee. Our purpose was not Christian education or family counseling, yet people were learning about life and they were reshaping relationships. In an apathetic group or organization people are playing it cool—learning how to stay out of touch with their feelings and their passions. This group was no longer apathetic. Rollo May says that apathy, not hate, is the opposite of love.[1] This is because apathy is indifference, a distancing and closing off of oneself from others. Love means reaching out and opening up the self, a commitment to affect and be affected by others. By not being just one more apathetic committee in which people buried their thoughts and feelings we had done far more than I had realized.

The parish has enormous power in people's lives. The issue is to take seriously that power, understand it, and use it for healing rather than for sickness. At its heart, to understand an organization or institution as a social system is to believe that in tortuously complex ways there are connections between a healthy organization and healthy people. Some of the simpler connections between an individual and the organization have been established by research. The omnipresent small group, at the informal and formal level, a major ingredient of every social system, has been clearly demonstrated to be a vital factor in the formation of human personality and behavior. The phrases, peer group and reference group are a part of the popular language of the day.

"For the individual the process through which a group becomes a reference group means forming attitudes derived from prevailing values, norms and practices for the group."[2]

I am acutely aware in my own life of the personal support which I draw from the small and closely allied group of colleagues with whom I work. They provide for me intellectual stimulation, personal security, political allies and a richer sense of myself in my work. I find it hard to imagine the personal cost if this group were to be dissolved.

In a classic study, E. L. Trist and K. W. Bamforth showed what happened to coal miners when their cohesive, small work groups were disrupted due to a technological change in the method of mining. Under the old method the men worked in an interdependent group of two to eight men. Mechanical equipment was brought into the mines which broke up these old, cohesive work groups into larger work shifts with the men separated physically and by increasing job specialization. The economic result was lower productivity. The human result was a high rate of absenteeism, sickness and psychosomatic disorders and a sense of indifference and loss of meaning.[3]

In an article on the socialization processes which an organization exerts on members, Dr. Edgar Schein of M. I. T. reports the shock experienced by executives who before promotion had condemned the business practices of their superiors but who after promotion were forced to cope with the same organizational pressures. He quotes one man as saying, "my ethical standards changed so gradually over the first five years of work that I hardly noticed it, but it was a great shock to suddenly realize what my feelings had been five years ago and how much they had changed."[4]

The strengthening and healing power possible in our group memberships was exemplified for me in one parish which has been quite self conscious about what it is teaching in the process by which people become members and which is concerned for the educational nature of people's total experience in that congregation. Two mornings a week this parish has a therapist from a community mental health agency available at a walk-in clinic in the parish hall. I interviewed the therapist to get her reflections on the climate of this congregation's life. She said that the staff of the mental health agency felt strongly that most of the patients normally seen by the agency were not a part of a cohesive, stable, social group. They lacked the assistance of a supportive group. She said she knew that in most congregations people turned to the pastor for counseling in times of crisis. What she noticed that was different in this parish, in contrast to the agency's usual experiences, was the way in which people felt a part of an on-going supportive network. "They feel a part of things and they feel they can get help from many different people." It is no accident that this parish works so hard to examine and stay in touch with the reality of wants and expectations, the nature of people's learnings about the parish—the whole fabric of education that occurs between an individual and the organization. It is a parish committed to continually sensing the reality of the needs, wants, and expectations which members bring to their participation in that congregation. The parish norm is to respect and respond to people where they are, not where someone thinks they ought to be. Their cohesion as a community is built on a network of trust which is the resultant of free and open communication.

THE NATURE OF A HEALTHY CLIMATE

As I have noted, a parish is a social system, a living environment which by the teaching of a thousand cumulative experiences tends to confirm or deny the identity of its people. Everything that happens in a congregation is religious education. For me the essential test of that teaching experience—the essence of both personal and organizational health is to be able to stay in touch with the reality of what is happening, to continually seek to understand that reality, and hence to respond in terms of the truth rather than a fantasy or distorted perception.

At some of the more neurotic moments in my life I found that I was responding to wishes I had for myself rather than to the reality of the emotions and perceptions I was experiencing. My wish to be helpful—

the sense that I ought to be able to do the right thing—led to renewed and redoubled efforts to be helpful and to a disregard of the messages that were saying I was overworked and allowing myself to be put upon by others. Organizations as well as individuals often carry within themselves these sets of unconscious "oughts," "musts," "shoulds," and "wishes," which lead to the organization ignoring the reality of the information it possesses about its behavior. I have seen Church boards operating under a collective sense that the Board ought to be helpful to the pastor and then seeing that Board grit its teeth to work "like crazy," ignoring all the while abundant information which said that they were poorly utilized, distrusted, and misused.

My own belief is that the major standard for a healthy organizational climate is whether or not the system rewards or punishes, supports or denies the actual facts of its ongoing life. Does the organization support a board member saying he is confused and doesn't understand what is happening or does the system treat such information as irrelevant and getting in the way of what we ought to be doing? Is a parish willing to take note of the reality that a majority of its members are apathetic or actually opposed to the social activist stance of the pastor and a small core group? Most organizations punish the truth.

Rather than an organizational ideal to be attained I regard this process of using the truth as a dynamic to continually be accomplished. The resolution of the problem of attaining a healthy climate is in a continual attention to the realities—the good and the bad; the trusting and untrusting; the healthy and unhealthy aspects of organizational life.

This climatic issue can be illustrated in several ways. Forty some men and women, clergy and laity representing several denominations, were into the second week of a training program to help them understand some of the organizational complexities of the church. The group was divided in two; one subgroup was asked to describe the characteristics of a healthy institution. What would be some of the attributes of an organization that provided an exciting and renewing climate for its people? The other group was asked to describe the attributes of the church as they knew it. The two groups returned and compared their lists.

A Healthy Organization	*The Church*
People's feelings are important.	Not to share feelings although such feelings are operating.
All norms open to examination.	Don't rock the boat.
Able to look at itself without realistically justifying or denouncing changes.	Answers to problems looked for in tradition and scripture.
Decision making close to the sources of information.	Decisions made on basis of how they meet the needs of small, inner core.
Broad base of ownership by members.	Meeting community inclusion needs, association needs, affiliation needs.
Persons external to the organization are useful.	Blaming, placating, rationalizing, avoiding as way of dealing with conflict. Legitimizes cultural preferences.
Conflict can be useful and is a given.	Passive, dependent behavior more acceptable than agressive-independent.

Looking at the lists one man said in a high, hard, tense voice, "Do you know the North Carolina state motto?" He said it reads, "It is better to be than to seem." Then he said, "I believe the church says it is better to seem than to be." Excitement and urgency swirled through the room. Over the energized noise of the conversation of this group of the church's most talented and capable leaders a voice cried, "But this is where the church really is!" In point of fact this is where most organizations are and the issue is to stay in touch with these realities rather than to spend our energies lamenting the problem. The real issue is not that there is a discrepancy between the Church as it exists and some "ideal" institution but rather in the fact that the Church too often acts so as to ignore the information it already possesses about its behavior.

THE EMPEROR'S CLOTHES

"It is better to seem than to be" can become a motto for the suppression of valid information about what is happening to people in an organization. The way in which this denial of reality can become characteristic of a whole social system is beautifully illustrated in the fairy tale about the emperor's new clothes, well known to most readers. To summarize two swindlers come to the kingdom of an Emperor who is slavishly devoted to fine clothing. They announce that they have developed a weave so fine that their fabrics are the most beautiful imaginable. Indeed, they are so superior as to be invisible to inferior persons, dull people, or those not fit for their callings in life. The Emperor sends his court officials to check on the wondrous cloth, and all alike are unable to handle the fact that they see nothing. "I know I am no fool," thought one man, "so it must be that I am unfit for my good post. It is very strange, though. However, one must not let it appear." As official after official praises the remarkable materials, the Emperor himself comes to believe that he must be a fool or unfit because he can not see them. The illusion gains more and more strength, royal garments are made of the elusive fabrics, and the Emperor goes on a grand procession through the streets attired in his grand new clothes. "None of the Emperor's clothes had been so successful before." Finally a child whispers that the Emperor is naked. The word rushes through the crowd until it reaches the Emperor himself, who realizes that it is true. But in an ending often forgotten, he draws himself up in even more regal pose and the procession continues with the court chamberlains marching on holding the hem of the Emperor's invisible clothing.

Anna Freud has helped us to see that the denial of disagreeable reality by the reversal of unwelcome facts in imagination is a part of a normal child's development. As a defense mechanism of the adult years, "it indicates an advanced stage of psychic disease."[6] If we were to analyze the fairy tale in a liberal vein, we would have to say that by defending themselves against the anxiety of possibly not being good enough, the people of the kingdom were betraying themselves until they were no longer free to choose the truth.

Dr. Chris Argyris of Harvard University has spent much of his professional life studying the psychological connections between the individual and organizations. He points out the blindness of—like that of the Emperor in his undress—organizational leaders to potentially threatening information. Business executives consistently say that they feel openness, trust and risk-taking are important; just as consistently such behavior is in fact rarely seen at their business meetings.

"In [one] study, eighteen officers of an organization described their superior's behavior as constricting, pressuring, dependence producing, and inhibiting of innovation. The superiors had predicted the opposite reports. Interestingly, the behavior of the eighteen subordinates was taped as they interacted with their superiors. Their behavior was as constricting and inhibiting as was their superior's behavior about which they complained."[7]

Argyris has found time and again that organizations have norms against avowing one's feelings, telling others about their personal impact on you, or allowing other people to express their feelings and values. The more threatening the information to individuals, groups, and the organization as a whole, the less likely it is ever to come to the surface. Hence, enormous discrepancies are perpetuated between what people say they believe and what actually happens. The information as to these discrepancies lies buried; the Emperor marches on with the courtiers supporting his imaginary train. Argyris tells of a group of business executives who explained the burial of their negative feelings toward one another as being due to their trust and respect for each other.[6] It is the same phenomenon I encountered not too long ago in the governing board of a congregation. Several members of the board said that the reason they would not tell the pastor of their anger and disappointment with him was because they loved him too much to hurt him. In the meantime, the pastor was growing more and more frantic trying to cope with an increasingly apathetic congregation.

A crucial difference for the church is that the institution promises, teaches, and tries to provide programs which will lead to personal renewal—to an inward learning of true ways of living. The result is that this suppression of personal feelings and valid information as to the actual state of people's perceptions is justified on the ultimate and symbolic ground of religious truth. I have found time and again that it matters very little what the preacher teaches from the pulpit about the importance of love, trust, caring, and empathy in the Christian fellowship. Far more important is the learning which comes from the actual behavior sanctioned by the social system. The behavioral norms—that is, the specific oughts or musts of behavior which are punished or rewarded in a thousand subtle ways by the organization—carry the real authority about the nature of Christian fellowship. It is here that the business of parish Christian education really takes place. Hence people have learned it is better to seem than to be. "It is better to seem interested in a board meeting than to deal with the reality that I am bored with the triviality of our work, the inept leadership of the meeting, the disruption and personal tragedy of the verbose, pompous, consistently half-drunk member. My fellow members seem interested—maybe it's just me. Maybe this is the way things ought to be and I am the only one feeling this way."

The authority of the institutional church resides in its capacity to invoke congruent insights, both symbolic and experiential, into the nature of existence. Our authority as the proclaimer of right doctrine is rapidly eroding; I hope it goes quickly. Jesus claimed that the Sabbath was made for man and not man for the Sabbath.[11] I take it he meant Truth must be embodied, incarnate in life, not in religious dogma. Truth is discerned in the embodied whole, the gestalt, the totality of the life of the social system, the church—not in the simple proclamation of right belief from pulpit and classroom. In a voluntary society where there is freedom of choice, the Emperor would eventually have trouble finding courtiers to hold up his nonexistent train. He marched firmly on because to believe in his clothes was to support the authority of empire. Without the coercive power of the institution—the empire—the belief that the clothes exist would lose a major support. Everything that happens in a congregation educates. The learning it is able to transmit is the result of the total experience of life in that congregation. The rituals of worship, the words of prayer and scripture, the architecture, the web of human relationships, the norms and roles and patterns of interaction, these and countless other factors form the curriculum of Christian education in the church context. These are the formative experiences influencing the communication of Truth.

Notes

1. Rollo May, *Love and Will* (New York: W. W. Norton & Co., 1969), p. 29.

2. Muzafer Sherif and Carolyn W. Sherif, *An Outline of Social Psychology* (New York: Harper & Row: 1956), p. 541.

3. E. L. Trist and K. W. Bamforth, "Some Social and Psychological Consequences of the Longwoll Method of Coal-getting," *Human Relations* (February 1951), pp. 3–38.

4. Edgar H. Schein, "Organizational Socialization and the Profession of Management," *Industrial Management Review* (Winter 1968), p. 8.

5. Hans Christian Andersen, *Andersen's Fairy Tales*, (New York: Grosset & Dunlap, 1945), pp. 263–68.

6. Anna Freud, *The Ego and the Mechanism of Defense* (New York: International University Press, 1946), p. 85.

7. Chris Argyris, *Intervention Theory and Method: A Behavioral Science View* (Reading, Mass.: Addison-Wesley Co., 1970), p. 75.

8. Ibid., p. 74.

9. Mark 2:27

8

Change

Can the Ethiopian change his skin or the leopard his spots?
—Jeremiah 13:23

GREAT EXPECTATIONS

I have spent a large share of my life concerned about change. I remember in sixth grade knowing that the change to Junior High School would mean at long last I was taking that first step into adolescence and things were really going to change. In Junior High I remember thinking that the forthcoming change to the high school would mean I had finally arrived. Early in life (as the reader will begin to see) I had a list in my mind, with the heading over it: Oh, how my life will be changed when

113

I (fill in the blank)! Living and growing up was the process of adding to this list and checking items off it.

Oh, how my life will be changed when I _____ !
    make the tennis team
    find a steady girl
    am accepted at college
    get through exams
    get to be twenty-one
    graduate from college
    am a husband and father
    get out of the Marine Corps
    am accepted in seminary
    graduate from seminary
    get ordained
    am my own boss

As events were added to the list and checked off as accomplished, I began to discover that there was something wrong with my hopes for change. I began to wonder when I would reach the point of really living rather than working on the list. It had been my belief that by putting the right things on it and working hard to see that they happened, life would at some golden moment become what it ought to be—I would have altered the shape of the human affairs of James Anderson until I found my rightful self. Human beings find it harder to pretend to immortality than do organizations; I began to realize something was amiss. The changes happened, but they didn't bring me what I wanted. An awful lot of life was slipping by while I continued to look for it. While I went on to searching for the right change, I had forgotten that I was changing all the time, growing older, adding gray hair, adding life experiences. I found that life was what I was living; if I kept trying to find it in the right changes it would elude me forever. What really needed to change was my process of living, not the circumstances of my life.

Now, I recognize that the whole world is not created in my compulsive image. Yet there is in my own history of misunderstanding a pattern which is repeated time and again when people in organizations think about organizational change. It is a crucial, commonplace, repetitive distortion of the nature of change in human affairs. The easiest way I can explain it is to say that people have a list in their minds which is headed: "Oh, how the organization will be changed when (fill in the blank) _____ !"

The most usual answers are:

(when) the new boss arrives
the reorganization is completed
we quit reorganizing and realize that nothing ever changes around here
we have enough members
we have enough money
we find our identity
we finally start planning
we finally stop planning and get to work
we find the right program

PERSPECTIVES ON CHANGE

The reader I assume is also concerned for change. He senses that in some way the institution is not functioning well and that some changes need to occur. He is looking for guidance about how that change might best take place.

My first advice is that it is absolutely necessary to look at change from the proper perspective. It is important to move beyond the common features of approach to change which I have characterized in the two lists. There is a sense in both that something is not going as well as it should. I am not happy with the way things are now, and they need to change. The source of that discontent is unexamined. A second feature of the two lists is that both regard change in a highly simplistic fashion as an effort to "add on" a new program, a new skill, a new curriculum, a new experience. "Well, we added on that new program and it didn't work—nothing ever changes around here." This is the wrong perspective. Real change began for me when I finally realized that what I needed to do was to get in touch with the roots of my discontent, understand more clearly the ever-changing processes of my life, see what each of the events of change had meant for me, and on the basis of this understanding take better charge of the ongoing flow of my life. The *basic* change problem for any social system is the extent to which it can *monitor and influence* the external and internal forces which are bringing unavoidable change. A person or a social system is continually changing. Change is in many ways synonymous with life. Some change is progress and some is regression. I suggest that we will be better off if we speak less about change and more about understanding the continuing interplay of forces at work in the life of an institution.

The "add-on-an-event" view of change is quite prevalent. There is some of it in all of us. Listen to the first change questions people often ask:

"Can you tell me what some other people are doing that works?"

"Our youth program hasn't worked for years. Do you think that new small-group plan would do?"

"Our committees never seem to get their work done—can you tell us a better way to organize?"

"Our church school is lousy—help us find the right curriculum!"

Searching for the "best" Christian Education program or the "best" way of organizing a vestry is fruitless and frustrating. The effectiveness of a system cannot be measured by the efficiency of its parts but rather is contained in the overall capacity of the system as it functions to accomplish its purpose. To speak of organizational change is a misnomer. The reality is that we are trying to talk and learn about organizations changing. Thus a systematic approach to change leads to initial questions which focus on trying to understand what is actually happening.

What do you understand to be the problem?
What is it you are trying to accomplish?
What do you see to be your most realistic opportunities?
Why do you want to change?
What are the forces that are preventing you from taking action?

In trying to change an organization such as a church or congregation we must remember that we are dealing with a social system and that the change process has to do with getting in touch with the living processes of the system and making clear choices about what can and cannot be influenced.

I want to use one more example to hammer this perspective home. Some social systems are easier to understand and more familiar to us than others—for example, a football team or a symphony orchestra. Imagine for a moment that the local congregation is analogous to a football team. A vestryman or deacon says, "Our board is poorly organized—we never seem to get the job done—people don't follow through, and it's hard to get volunteers. We need to reorganize." Translating this statement for the analogy, it is as if someone on a losing football team said, "We're having a terrible season, the players are losing their team spirit—we need to reorganize. We've used the 'T' formation too long."

Now, because an athletic team is a relatively simple social system with highly structured roles and patterns of interaction it is easier to see the fallacy of the approach. The type of organization used by a football team is only one small aspect of the system. We can all see that the change from a losing to a winning ball club involves a complex and highly interrelated set of forces. A partial list would include:

> the knowledge and skill of the coaching staff
> the personal authority of the head coach
> the climate of team spirit
> the native athletic ability of the players

the quality of the skill training of individual players
the quantity and quality of team practices
the ability of players and coaches to learn from feed-
    back provided by game films and coaching staff
the timing and coordination of individual plays
the interpersonal relations among players and coaches
the quality of the equipment and playing field
the accuracy of scouting reports on the opposition
the strength of the opposing teams

There is enough complexity and interaction to these dynamics so that no one can be certain of putting together a winning ball club. One thing we can be sure of is that if we tried to build winning football teams with as simplistic a view as is commonly used to build winning organizations there would be far fewer fall weekends spent watching this national sport. Why should one small working committee of twelve people be any easier to create than one twelve-man football squad. It is, in fact, at least as difficult to build a spirited, skilled problem-solving group, yet we continually assume it will happen without training, skill, practice, feedback, or time and energy devoted to the task. The skills needed by a football team are relatively easy to identify. Work groups are not used to thinking in skill terms about their team problem. An organization is typically made up of many such groups which must interrelate with one another. Not only must each work team be effective; they must also learn how to work well with other teams and levels of the organization.

The Alcoholics Anonymous prayer expresses in petition form the perspective on organizational change I am advocating.

God grant me the serenity
To accept the things I cannot change,
Courage to change the things I can,
And wisdom to know the difference.[1]

Serenity, courage, and wisdom belong together in an organizational change effort. Looking at the church, there are certainly groups possessing large amounts of serenity, and in recent years several with great courage for making changes. Our shortage has been of those who approach our institutional dilemmas with respect for all aspects of this beautiful prayer.

Wisdom in particular has been in short supply. The institutional tendency in the last two years or so has been to turn to the literature on organization change as one might turn to a catalog for a set of new program gimmicks. Organization change and development are fast becoming a fad. It will fail. If organization development is used as a new program to revitalize the church it will be a loser. This is simply adding the use of this technology onto the list of right changes: "This organization will really change when—it begins to use OD." I doubt it.

Let us look more closely at the nature of organization development, or OD. This is a relatively new technology of organizational change. It represents a synthesis of learnings from social psychology, management training and human relations training. Basically a problem-solving approach, it uses the services of a trained consultant to help the organization identify its problem accurately, diagnose analytically what is going wrong, and solve the systemic problems through strategies which rely heavily, but not totally, on the human factors of organizational life. The consultant's role is to help the organization over a period of time to increase its inherent capability of moving through the problem-solving cycle. The perspective for problem identification is a view of the organization as an open sociotechnical system—that is, as a dynamic whole in which the means of production, the ways people interact, and the interface with the environment must be viewed as one cultural entity. Richard Beckhard states the basic position of the OD consultant as being: "How can we optimally mobilize the human resources and energy to achieve the organization's mission and at the same time maintain a viable growing organization of people whose personal needs for self worth, growth, and satisfaction are significantly met at work."[2]

Numerous books and aritcles are available which spell out OD technology in detail.[3] That is not my intention in this book. I would like to suggest that organization development is related to institutional renewal as psychoanalysis is to mental health. It would be foolish to think that psychoanalysis is a cure-all for the mental health problems of this country or the world. The problem is far too large and complex to be solved by this one expensive, time-consuming, narrowly specialized approach. Nevertheless, the entire field of mental health and the nature of our knowledge of the human psyche is deeply in debt to psychoanalysis. It is a therapeutic approach which can be characterized as applied research into the depths of personal existence. In a similar fashion, organization development is an organizational therapy based on applied research into the depths of corporate existence. We are rapidly becoming indebted to OD as the field for development of knowledge about how social systems operate. The earlier chapters of this book have been worked up out of personal experiences as an OD consultant and the experience of others in the OD phase of the research of Project Test Pattern. This does not mean that OD is the answer to institutional renewal for the church or any other organization. To make it into a program fad is foolishly to disregard the complex realities of organizational life. But to ignore the proper use of OD and the learnings flowing from it is to turn our backs on wisdom.

Most of the literature on organizational change is written from or addressed to the point of view of an external change agent. It is heavily focused on the role of the outside consultant and the processes he uses to facilitate change. The person who works within the institution (as manager, consultant, or staff person) finds he must translate the writings if they are to have relevance for him In addition, what has been written on the change process invariably describes stages or phases of it. The person working with the dilemmas of everyday institutional life finds it hard to recognize his problems in a list of phases consisting of such items such as "establishing the change relationship" or "unfreezing the system."

A DETAILED VIEW

To avoid being trapped in the depths of this translation problem I want to take a typical issue of change in a congregation and use it to highlight what I believe are the significant practical and theoretical problems involved. Parish Y is having difficulty with its entire youth program. The Sunday school from seventh grade up has had sparse attendance at a time when the rest of the church school was showing marked improvement. An attempt was made to turn over a great deal of the direction and control of the Sunday evening church group to the young people The effort failed and the program sputtered to a halt.

This is literally a jewel of a problem By looking at its many facets I believe we shall be able to recognize the wide variety of ways of understanding the change problems involved and the complementary validity of each means of exploring them.

The first way the clergy of Parish Y looked at the problem was to ask, "Does someone else have a program that works?" It is my experience that this is often the initial formation of the problem. Here is what that question means for the social system (see diagram). If the diagram seems ambitious to you, at the very least the question the clergy are asking is, "Has some church somewhere stumbled on a program which seems to be attractive to young people, and is there any person, group, or agency who knows about the program, and can we make contact with them or their information?" No matter how you slice it the question implies that somewhere, somehow, the total social system is generating new knowledge in the form of new programs, and that the system has communication processes and organizational linkage so that this knowledge has some chance of being spread widely throughout the organization. Viewed from this angle these questions are the basic change issues. For one denomination—the Protestant Episcopal—here is the shape of those issues.

There is an annual notebook published in collaboration with five other denominations.[4] It is a collection of successful youth ministry programs. The notebook also refers the reader to other source newsletters and periodicals which (from time to time) contain similar success stories and program hints. The Episcopal Church has no funding or personnel at the national level for basic or applied research in work with youth. It has one staff person for the entire field of Christian education. A part of that

Initial Formulation of the Problem

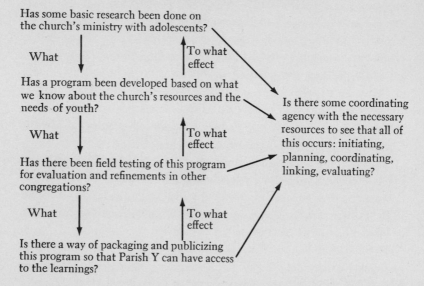

Has some basic research been done on
the church's ministry with adolescents?

What | To what effect

Has a program been developed based on what
we know about the church's resources and the
needs of youth?

What | To what effect

Is there some coordinating
agency with the necessary
resources to see that all of
this occurs: initiating,
planning, coordinating,
linking, evaluating?

Has there been field testing of this program
for evaluation and refinements in other
congregations?

What | To what effect

Is there a way of packaging and publicizing
this program so that Parish Y can have access
to the learnings?

individual's job is to see to it that the Youth Ministry notebook is compiled and written. Some funding has been available each year to support local youth programs which seemed to be innovative or experimental. At the regional or diocesan level Parish Y can turn to one individual again responsible for the entire field of Christian education, whose offices are at the other end of the state three hundred miles away. The regional situation does differ from one locale to another. If Parish Y were located in some other area of the country, they might find from none to three regional staff people. The region may have a central office which has a comprehensive display or library of educational resources. There might be a regional resource newsletter and occasional regional workshops designed to provide information about innovative models. Parish Y did send two people to a week-long workshop this past summer.

Parish Y has an adequate physical plant. One room is used as an educational resource library. The clergy state that some of the back issues of the Youth Ministry notebook are probably filed in the resource library (the new notebook has not arrived). The laity are unfamiliar with the resource room and the notebook. No one can be found who is familiar with the youth notebooks or the two resource newsletters to which the parish subscribes. In other words the parish's internal processes for the diffusion of knowledge are as spare and ineffective as the processes on the regional and national level.

The most likely place for the parish to gain new information is through the clergy informally swapping ideas about what seems to work. Certain clergy in the region are opinion leaders who are quick to try innovations, and whose evaluation is highly credible to their peers. This process has been researched elsewhere in such areas as the way doctors adopt a new drug or farmers a new hybrid seed technique.[5] In no region, so far as I know, is there an organized effort to harness this process in a self-conscious diffusion effort for the church.

The first change issue, then, is that at all levels of the system—local, regional, and national—there are few resources allocated to the generation and distribution of new knowledge, and few procedures or structures for that purpose. The deliberate planning of basic research, applied research, and field testing is terribly expensive and almost nonexistent. The channels for the distribution of information that do exist are narrow and overworked or ineffective.

The parish also has to ask itself what is the priority of youth work. As a goal for this congregation is it widely shared, and are people genuinely committed to it? Because of previous work done to monitor the nature of the stake people have in the parish and because of previous goal-setting activity, the leadership can answer Yes to these questions. Accordingly, they decide to allocate substantial funds to support their entire Christian education program, including youth work. On the basis of this prior work it is decided to use part of the money to hire a moonlighting resource person from the national level. The parish is using its own money to lay down a direct hot line to the information and to bring into the local situation a person whose everyday work keeps him in touch with some of the programs that really work.

The second formulation of the change issues by the clergy and key laity of Parish Y was, "We have tried the Youth Notebook before and had trouble fitting it to our situation. Some of the things sounded like good ideas, but they didn't seem to work well for us." From this facet the systemic change issues are: Can the user (Parish Y) correctly diagnose its own situation so as to know the type of solution, information, or program for which it is looking? Does the user have the capacity to consider the implications of each alternative? Does the using system have the capacity to install a solution for a trial period and evaluate and modify the program? Are there resources at the regional or national level to assist the parish in making a correct diagnosis and in choosing, installing, evaluating, and modifying the best alternative? Is the knowledge made available in such a fashion as to facilitate these decisions?

This second facet of the change issues can be explained by an analogy. It is as if a homeowner is having problems with his dishwasher. The dishes just aren't coming out clean. He does have some information available to him about a whole new line of dishwashers that really sound great. He buys one, tries to install it himself, runs into a lot of plumbing and wiring trouble, finally gets it running, and the dishes are still dirty. The homeowner says, "I've tried the dishwashers out of that catalog before; they looked good but didn't work well for us. Systemically speaking, the fact is that the dishwasher is a part of several significant subsystems in that house, such as the electrical system and the plumbing and hot water systems. The problem could just as well have been in the hot water system as in the dishwasher. Or was the user helped to see that the type of dishwasher and detergent chosen should take into account the chemical and mineral content of local water? The homeowner, digging more deeply, finds that the dishwasher distributor is not at all equipped to help him make the proper choice or to assist him with the installation of the appliance.

The analogy almost exactly describes the situation of Parish Y with regard to the second set of change issues. At least two serious problems were involved in the earlier failure of youth programing, which at first were not considered by the leadership. These were (1) confusion among the leadership regarding their respective role relationships in the program, and (2) a lack of skill and knowledge in the leadership concerning work with young people. The parish had almost no structure for and very little skill in diagnosing the problems. The same structures and skills were missing for installation, so new problems arose in trying out the programs. The written success story format of the resources was of little help when difficulties arose. The one resource person at the diocesan level seemed too remote to be of real assistance. Moreover, they were not sure what was going wrong and so it was hard to ask for help.

Parish Y resolved these questions by further utilization of the outside resource people, whom it had hired on a retainer basis. With their help a more complete diagnosis was made of the earlier frustrating program. A lay committee was formed, combining young and old to guide the youth program. The role of the committee and its members was carefully delineated. The assistant rector's designated role with the group was to help it become a working team. Some training and assistance in program-planning skills was given to the group by one of the outside consultants.

The next statement of the change problem by the clergy and Youth Committee of Parish Y was, "The program we think we want may cause some conflict. It will mean youth becoming a genuine and equal part of Sunday morning worship, in what we have called the adult education time. There may also be trouble on two other points. We have people who are excited about the Jesus movement—pro and con—that is fast becoming an issue. Second, this is a suburban ghetto—we live very isolated lives here, and the community is extremely fearful about many aspects of the youth movement. We may run headlong into this community fear about drugs and sexual license."

The change dynamics are now growing wider and more complex. The committee senses possible conflict within the congregation and with the community over the program direction they are favoring, which involves working with youth to organize around issues of concern to the youth themselves. One such question is that of dress and hair codes at the high school. Systemic conditons brought into focus at this stage are multiple and interlocking. First, there is the relationship of the parish to the community. In the past the parish has clearly served to support and inform the values of the community. This has been the traditional function of this rather elderly congregation in its prestigious suburban location. The youth committee is largely composed of a new breed of community inhabitant—younger, less affluent, without the old-line social connections of the power people in town and in the congregation. The make-up of the congregation itself is almost evenly divided between the new mobile families living on the developing fringes and long-established residents of the town.

A second major change dynamic is the parish norm about conflict. Past rectors have chosen to use the wealth and power of the parish and community by being careful not to rock the boat. The parish is valued as a tranquil, stable, conserver of values. Conflict, in fact differences of any kind, disturb the ordered security for which this congregation has historically been known. Even the new families who now live on the outskirts of town were at first not greeted with great enthusiasm. The parish is not used to fighting, it is not used to differences, and neither is valued.

The rector is not afraid of conflict. He believes deeply that the parish needs to move toward pluralism. He is convinced that if enough trust can be built and a pluralistic congregation emerges, the church will be exercising a prophetic ministry to this community.

A new resource is discovered and the die is cast. Through the clergy grapevine the rector hears of a young man working at the metropolitan YMCA. He is a conscientious objector doing his alternate service. Bright, attractive, skilled, interested in working part time with a local congregation, this young man captivates the Youth Committee and they move ahead with their program. Simultaneously, the rector decides to do all that he can to change the parish conflict norm. Knowing that the vestry contains some of the key opinion leaders in the congregation and believing that strong vestries makes strong rectors, he decides to begin with this group.

Drawing on their contractual relationship with the national staff person, a weekend conference is held for the vestry with the staff person in the role of consultant. By grace or fate this conference occurs just as the parish realizes that it will probably be visited by a militant black power group demanding reparation money. This becomes the major issue of the weekend. The vestry is torn by furious debate. One of the vestrymen unlocks the argument by asking a member of the opposition what *values* he feels will be destroyed if the black militants are allowed to enter the worship service. Using this question, the vestry clarifies its value differences and finds that those opposed to an open reception of the black power group in the worship service have no objection if the meeting is held in the parish hall. The value differences turn out to be the appropriateness of the liturgy and the sanctuary as the setting for political confrontation. Triumphant over its ability to move creatively through a bitter conflict, the vestry emerges from the weekend with a decision to invite the black militants to the parish hall on a Sunday following the services. The meeting is held. Its outcome is described as "indifferent."

Eighteen months later the youth program has disappeared in a flurry of controversy. The youthful YMCA worker created a large, excited following of young people, but their activities in the local high school generated so much controversy that a decision was made by the rector and vestry to let the group die a natural death. The services of the youth worker were not engaged for a second year.

Within the vestry a slight shift in the conflict norm has continued. There is greater willingness to own differences, and less flight from controversy into rational abstractions. This is still not true of most parish groups or the congregation as a whole.

The youth group experience has educated the leadership regarding the strength of the collective esteem with which the parish's role as conserver of traditional family values is regarded. The fragmentation of these values in the culture is increasing the importance of this expectation for a majority of the congregation.

The eighteen-month period has also seen a continued influx of new families into the parish. The old social elite of the town are now outnumbered by transient young families. As the rector muses on the present situation he asks, "How can we handle the differences in values between these two groups? Parish committees are still largely controlled by the old elite. They continue to want their way. When I loaded the Youth Committee with new folk they ended up doing things, 'their way.' The vestry has been some help, but it is too taken up with housekeeping and Robert's Rules at its regular meetings to really get into these things."

Working with the parish's outside consultant resource person, the rector takes these questions to the vestry and information is developed collectively to illuminate the organizational processes involved in these various differences. It becomes clear that the vestry's procedures for doing its work are inadequate. They recognize that their tidy system of committees and committee reports to be voted up or down by the vestry as a whole is failing. Many of the new people in the congregation show little interest in being part of such a cumbersome, time-consuming, multi-layered organization. The vestry remember with excitement the way it was able to dig into the black power issue. They begin to recognize a distinction between the kinds of work procedures that facilitate program development and evaluation—the kind of work a management task force does—and their usual style, based upon the formalized deliberations of a legislative body.

Decisions are made to have only four meetings a year as a legal-legislative body, passing on finances and property details. The other six meetings are to be carefully structured so that initiative may be taken on some of the substantive issues of congregational life. The first is set to explore ways in which the old power elite and new suburban dwellers can work toward a pluralistic accommodation. One specific to be addressed is the way nominations to the vestry have been closely controlled by the incumbent vestry. The rector asks that the second meeting be devoted to examining the processes by which parish goal-setting is carried out. He feels that the differences in personal goals held by constituent elements in the congregation demand more adequate participatory goal-setting procedures and greater clarity and awareness of goals. In private the rector says he believes there will be some resistance to this, since those who are satisfied with things as they are view going along with implicit goals as a way of keeping things as they have always been.

A year later, at its now annual conference, the vestry reflects on the changes it has made with considerable pride. A new goal-setting procedure has come into being and several vestry committees have disappeared. The committees that do exist are tied to the goals. There is an increasing tendency by clergy and vestry to adopt a facilitating, coordinating style of organization. As one man puts it, "We believe that anybody who has an idea should be helped to organize to do it. A bureaucratic structure of committees just didn't work. We spent too much time in the past worrying over our authority as a vestry—heavyhanded supervision. We are learning to listen to what people really want to do and set them free to do it." The rector jumps in and adds that he believes these changes are contributing to greater respect for pluralism. "The parish has a women's consciousness-raising group. Those who wanted it were delighted that I would help get it started, but were even more pleased when *I* was delighted that they kicked me out after the first meeting. It really surprised people to be rewarded for taking the initiative."

Parish Y does not exist. It is a composite of several congregations and people, but its story could go on for many more years. Better than any tidy list, I believe Parish Y illustrates many of my learnings about the process of change. Some of these are more questions than answers, but I do not apologize for that fact.

SUMMARY

I have tried to illustrate in Parish Y that:

1. To speak of change or a change agent is misleading. To use the language and categories of Dr. Chris Argyris, the task is to help the congregation (a) develop valid information about itself as an open social system; (b) create conditions in which congregational members may exercise free choice about the decisions that face them; and (c) create

conditions in which there may be genuine commitment or ownership
in the choices made.[6]

Information, choice, and commitment are core processes continually
operating as the system continually changes. It is a way of saying that
the basic change issue is the capacity of the system to monitor and
influence the external and internal forces that constitute the flow of life
in the organization. This is why the vestry of Parish Y found it made
more sense to spend time evaluating than supervising.

2. The rector is the key person in the local congregation. He is both
most influenced by and most influential upon the systemic norm. He
must be willing to examine the impact of his own behavior on the system
and learn from it. The pastor of Parish Y might have lost everything by
taking the youth program conflict as a personal failure or as the opening
gun of a vendetta with parish conservatives. Instead, he chose to learn
from what had happened. At the same time he is a man of personal
authority, a vigorous, live intelligent person. His willingness to learn does
not get read as personal ambivalence.

3. All the leadership did not come from the clergy. A core of competent, committed laity also willing to examine their own behavior was
indispensable to Parish Y. This is always true.

4. The processes involved in the revitalization of a congregation are
long-term, complex, and systemic in nature. Dimly discernible in the
functioning of Parish Y are the connections between the theology of the
rector, his goals for the congregation, the interaction with the values of
the community, and the impact on the role of the vestry of the effect
of these community changes on the parish. Moreover, I have tried to
show that Parish Y exists as part of a larger system. If it had not had
sufficient funds to hire outside assistance, the planned, deliberate efforts
to help the congregation cope with itself and its community would
probably not have occurred. These other levels of the institution were
not able to provide the support needed by Parish Y. The renewal of a
local congregation must be seen in the context of its place in a judicatory
and in a denomination. One may speculate, for instance, as to what it
would have meant to the rector of Parish Y to have heard grapevine

rumors of displeasure on the part of his ecclesiastical superiors over the youth program controversy.

5. I have attempted in Parish Y to show that the processes and elements of a congregation considered in more detail in earlier chapters (leadership, the psychological contract, role relations, reaction to differences, behavioral norms) are crucial, functional slices of parish life. They are aspects of that life where we begin to understand what is happening and hence are beginning to find the means to shape it.

6. A faddish, short-term, single-faceted approach to parish vitality will likely fail. Not all change is good. Some leaves the patient sicker than before treatment began. Some changes last for a few days, others for several years. If a man says to me, "Look, I'm using this new fertilizer on my fields—see how the seeds are growing!" I might be wise to reply, "Let me know the results in five years. Has the fertilizer killed the natural processes of the soil? Do you have to use more and more each year?" Who is to say that the work procedures and organizational design created by Parish Y are univerally true for all congregations? If you do you are mistaken. Parish Y—like any parish—is unique in its situation. It will not be helped by faddish reliance on any of the nostrums of recent years. "Human relations training, for one and all."—"Parish planning is the answer."—"Liturgical reform is the key to vitality."—"Try organizing a parish council." "What you need is organization development." —the slogans are traps. Parish Y is a mystery of infinite complexity. There will be no overnight magic miracles of renewal. Serenity, courage, and wisdom were and are what really counts in Parish Y.

7. Although not half so crucial as the rector and key laity, Parish Y did use the important services of an organization development consultant. This in itself is an innovation. It is my observation that a normative use of outside consultants and resource persons is becoming one of the hallmarks of congregations that cope well with themselves and their community.

8. Parish Y learned to repeat, continuallly and helpfully, a simple two-step cycle.

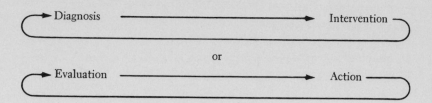

The cycle may be elaborated to a several-stage sequence so long as you realize it rarely happens in neat sequential order.

1. Data gathering
2. Problem identification
3. Problem analysis
4. Search for alternatives
5. Action
6. Evaluation

Part of the change in Parish *Y* is that as it became more practical and skilled at these steps, it developed enough trust so that candid information was easier to generate, and learned to go through these steps closer and closer to those actually involved in the doing.

One way of saying it is that the social system went to school and learned how to learn.

1. Attributed to Reinhold Niebuhr as quoted in Howard J. Clinebell, *Understanding and Counseling the Alcoholic* (New York: Abingdon Press, 1956), p. 143.

2. Richard Beckhard, *Organization Development, Strategies and Models* (Reading, Mass.: Addison-Wesley Co., 1969), p. 2.

3. Richard Beckhard, *Organization Development: Strategies and Models;* Warren Bennis, *Organization Development: Its Nature, Origins, and Prospects;* Christ Argyris, *Intervention Theory and Method: A Behavioral Science View* (Reading, Mass.: Addison-Wesley Co.) and W.W. Burke and H.A. Hornstein, *The Social Technology of Organization Development* (Washington, D.C.: NTL Institute).

4. *Youth Ministry Notebook V*, edited by Robert Theron Browne, was prepared for use in the Church of the Brethren, The Christian Church, The Episcopal Church, the Presbyterian Church in the U.S., the United Church of Christ, and the United Presbyterian Church in the United States of America. (New York: Seabury Press, 1971).

5. E. Rogers, *The Diffusion of Innovation*.

6. Chris Argyris, *The Invention Theory and Method: A Behavioral Science View*, (Reading, Mass.: Addison-Wesley Co., 1970).

9

A Larger View

As I look at the church and at the other great institutions in society I
see them struggling to cope with two central problems which cannot be
separated. They are systemically related, they feed each other. These
two problems are the shift in sources of authority and the fragmentation
of our cultural sources of meaning. Authority is no longer automatically
attached to or assumed by our institutions. More and more, people ask
if the Emperor's new clothes are real or not. From the family to the
president of a university to the regional archbishop, authority is no
longer easily accepted as conferred by mere position or office. The
institution must increasingly earn its authority by the nature of its
instrumental relationship to people's lives.

The second problem is that we all live in a frothing sea of ideological confusion. Unifying cultural constructs of meaning are nonexistent. There is a loss of authority in the rules by which we live. What are your values—how do you make sense of child-rearing, violence and nonviolence, respect for law, the role of religion in politics, educational practices, minority group quota? The list of discordant value problems is endless. There are no culturally compelling guidelines for living. Our myths and rituals no longer unite us, for the systems of meaning of which they are the expression are broken and fragmented. Our institutions have been referees in the game of life. Now they ask us, How do we referee when our authority is not respected and no one agrees on the rules?

I believe it is important to realize that man's longing for a sense of ultimate trust—to know and be known—has not changed. The structures of values, beliefs, and ethics and the structures of organized institutions are going through a time in the wilderness. Like the Israelites, we look for a way to turn back or someone to blame. "Were there no graves in Egypt, that you should have brought us here to die in the wilderness? See what you have done to us by bringing us out of Egypt! Is not this just what we meant when we said in Egypt, 'Leave us alone; let us be slaves to the Egyptians'?" (Ex. 14:11–12)

The hope of greater freedom on the far side of the desert is small comfort to us who live in terror of the day. The security of old tyrannies —mythical or institutional—can look very attractive while we wander in a barren wasteland.

ADAPT OR PERISH

The famed New Zealand teacher and writer Sylvia Ashton-Warner has published an account of her recent experiences teaching in a free school in this country. She vividly describes the shock of functioning sensitively in an educational institution today.

... one day in the autumn, I go straight from the plane into a foreign school of a culture I thought I knew. I'm agog with confidence in my own work, knowing it like ABC, but not knowing that I, from the tail end of civilization, have descended upon the spearpoint. True I have lived in other countries at varying stages of civilization, so that I know what civilization is and what a stage of civilization is, but here, in no time the days are a matter of survival and my work is XYZ. There's no time space or mind space to remember romantic conceptions of life about being a wandering exile or to dream about the stars. My comfortable principle of life—"Ask of no man but give to all" fails in the face of survival. My new watchword, clumsily assembled becomes—"Adapt and survive."[1]

There is no going back. There is much to lose in using our energies to blame the authorities for the situation. It will be easy in this time of wilderness freedom to turn to false gods—new idols. We can die in the wilderness, and many of us will. Some few in our society seem able to live as nomads, a romantic, wandering existence. Most of us cannot; but to survive is to adapt. The institutions that will survive must learn to adapt.

There is a wonderfully creative and interesting school in the community where I live. It now functions in an open classroom, free-school style with a young, bright, and lively faculty. At its best, the school is a vision of the human dream—at its worst, formless chaos. A small group of four-year-olds sitting for an hour and a half wrapped in the miracle of the emergent, triumphant, dazzling beauty of a monarch butterfly, soaring to join the migrating flight—a librarian almost frantic with the frustration of her inability to cope with 11- and 12-year-old girls who have no respect for her authority and who wander aimlessly from the library to the disordered freedom of their open classroom—a large, colorful, many-alcoved room in which a wondrous variety of children are variously clustered, huddled, seeking, discovering, shaping, exploring, testing the concepts of math, the lessons of history, the limits of their unfettered imaginations—a sizable group of parents who withdraw their children because they perceive that license rather than freedom is the order of the day and that their child has learned to play basketball rather than to read—two young male teachers working with primary-age children sharing with one another their educational dreams, their love for these children, their belief that here these visions can be realized—the growth of suspicion and frustration among faculty in sub-rosa discussion of their fragmented, divided understanding of what is "out-of-bounds" behavior by the children.

The school is struggling to cope, to adapt so as to survive. It cannot rely on the old sources of authority. The cultural ethic, baptized as Judeo-Christian—don't hassle your mother, father, or schoolteacher— doesn't work. Parents arrive with divided loyalties, values, and expectations. "I want my child to learn to think for himself, I am against rote education but I want him to be able to get into a good college." The four-walled, closed-door isolation of the traditional classroom is gone. Room passes, hall monitors, the line-up to proceed to the next class— all these tidy arrangements of the days in Egypt have vanished. For pupil, for teacher, and for parent the old assumed expectations of the role of each—teacher tell, pupil listen and practice, parent support—no longer serve as adequate stage directions for the drama of their life together. A teacher says, "The children will only respect us if we respect ourselves, respect them and respect one another. They don't give me respect just because I am a teacher." To adapt and cope, the school finds it must invent a new and more dynamic form of structure, a structure not of static rules and mechanisms—not of sanitized concrete and tile —but rather a building of trust between human beings, to hold open channels of candid communication. The school finds it must create normative, expected processes so that the teachers may explore their differences, develop curriculum, coordinate their work. A stability of regular interaction between parents, faculty, and staff is needed to sustain a learning climate for the school. Painfully the administration learns how to learn about the stormy, confusing social system which it must lead and try to influence. They have no way to transform our culture or turn the clock back on the directions in which educational institutions have moved. What they can and do do is to try to monitor—to understand the complexity with greater wisdom—and to create a new form of stability wherein problems whatever their shape can be identified, explored, worked on, and worked on again. A stability based on a consensus of trust in the processes by which work will be accomplished.

The labors of the church to adapt and survive are certainly as painful as the travail of educational institutions. The longer I live in the church and work with other institutions the more convinced I am that there is a wholeness to life which we ignore at our peril. Thought and action, theology and sociology, the individual and the group are systemically wedded. It is totally misleading to see our institutional problems as *(a)* needing to make Christian symbols relevant to a secular culture; *(b)* needing to apply sociological concepts so as to create a new secularized, therapeutic brand of Christianity. In point of fact, I believe our theological crisis can be understood as sociological in origin, or our sociological problem may be seen as theological in origin. Both the ancient Hebrew and today's system theorists recognize the mistake in dividing substance and form. It is not possible to understand the Old Testament if we read it with the rational, linear logic we have inherited in Western culture from the Greeks. Thus Western man persists in understanding the biblical concept of soul as being that special divine spark or substance in each human being which is God's special area of concern. In fact the biblical writers are speaking of the totality of a human being with the word "soul." Soul is the gestalt, the seen and unseen total or uniqueness of a person.[2]

The Israelite view of the unity of life was extended to the nation and culture as well. For them the soul of the person and the soul of the nation were as one. The Israelite had a sense of history because he was one with the cumulative experiences that shaped the whole—the gestalt of the land of his fathers. "To them a people is not a collection of human beings more or less like each other. It is a psychical whole, and in so far an ideal quantity. The 'people' is not visible. All common experiences are merged into the common soul and lend to it shape and fullness. Thus a psychic shock is created which is taken over from generation to generation, being constantly renewed and influenced by new experiences."[3]

I am not able to spell out in logical one-two-three fashion at each point the connections between organizational practices, theological concepts, and personal belief. On the basis of all I can read and understand psychologically, sociologically, and theologically I believe with biblical man that they constitute a whole. Unfortunately the institution does little to learn *how to learn* about this totality. A primary theological and organizational problem is that the ideological system that actually operates does not value this wholeness. Our organizational ideologies generally stress the separation of reason from emotion, the person in his wholeness from his work, his work from his home, his values from his efficiency, past history from the present. It does as much for this theological confusion to begin to clarify the situation organizationally as it would to somehow achieve theological clarity and consensus. Starting at either end—hopefully at both—is a way to begin to move on this enormously difficult problem. The point is that this characteristic of our ideological system impeded a commitment to learning and knowledge about ourselves as a social system.

Recently I had lunch with a fellow organization development consultant who directs the Organization Development efforts of a large American organization. I was describing some work I had done with a Church board. I had asked the individual board members to state their beliefs or values about a number of areas of social and organizational concern to the parish, such as abortion, ecology, the role of the laity and money. I told my friend that one board member had commented that this was the first time he had ever been asked in a church to talk about his personal values. My friend mused over this story commenting that he himself certainly would like to look to the Church as the place where he could work on questions of morals and values and yet he didn't expect to find the opportunity present in the institution. Then he said—"I guess that is the way with all organizations. It reminds me of a talk I had the other day with one of our branches where we have begun an organization development effort. I met with the branch manager who looked at me during the meeting and said with surprise—"It has been a long time in this company since we talked about people."

Are organizations made for man, or are men made for organizations? Can we learn in St. Paul's words to "discern the body" so that our organizational practices are not to our damnation?" (I Corinthians 11:- 29)

St. Paul on his missionary journeys acted as a roving consultant to the young struggling Christian enterprise. He helped these new congregations to sort out the roles of their leaders, to live with the conflicts created by their differences. He tried to help these groups to relate themselves to their communities. He aided the missions in their struggle to create organizational practices that were congruent with the values of their faith so that their daily practices might be a living witness. From the cauldron of these experiences was born the letters of advice and reflection which later generations have canonized into the theology of St. Paul. Unfortunately the Church for too long has paid more attention to St. Paul's words than to the realities of which he spoke.

For the system to be a learner, its existence must be tied to a stance of truthfulness: a learner's stance toward itself and the world. Paul Tillich has suggested that the Protestant principle is that Truth in the ultimate sense belongs only to God not man. Idolatry consists of submission to any man's or institution's claim to possess ultimate reality. "[This principle] is the critical guardian which protects the holy against the temptation of the bearers of the holy to claim absoluteness for themselves."[4] Our institutions are the expression of man's need to universalize his hopes and wishes for this world. Tillich reminds us of the fallacy of confusing the wish with reality. The church should be the first place where this fallacy is recognized—the last place to confuse the hope of the Kingdom of God with the actual life and work of the institution. When a social system lives by Tillich's Protestant principle it opens its whole life and functioning to a constant search for clearer understanding of what is happening to that institution—to its people and with the world about it.

The institution is the frontier. It is the frontier that brings to earth man's dream that all men are created equal, that men have unalienable rights basic to the created order. No institution can ever perfectly embody these truths in its beliefs and practices. However, it can learn to embody truthfulness: a stance of candor and a continuous search and inquiry for deeper wisdom and for fuller understanding.

Notes

1. Sylvia Ashton-Warner, "Spearpoint," *Saturday Review*, June 24, 1972, pp. 33–39.

2. Pedersen Johs, *Israel Its Life and Culture*, (London: Oxford University Press, 1926), p. 101.

3. Ibid., p. 475.

4. Paul Tillich, *Systematic Theology*, three volumes in one (New York: Harper & Row, 1967), 1:227.

74 75 76 77 10 9 8 7 6 5 4 3 2